s'mores cereal treats

snow cones

avocado toast

asian nachos

blt chopped salad

ultimate Dining Hall HACKS

DESSERTS · BREAKFAST · SALADS · SANDWICHES · PASTAS · ANYTIME MEALS · SNACKS

chicken pot pie

spinach-artichoke melt

teriyaki pasta

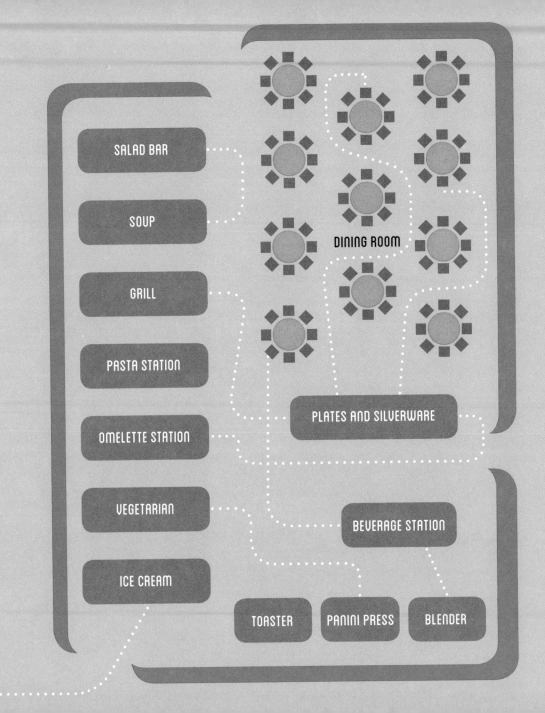

SALAD BAR

SOUP

GRILL

PASTA STATION

OMELETTE STATION

VEGETARIAN

ICE CREAM

DINING ROOM

PLATES AND SILVERWARE

BEVERAGE STATION

TOASTER   PANINI PRESS   BLENDER

Create
Extraordinary
Dishes from
the Ordinary
Ingredients in
Your College
Meal Plan

ultimate
Dining
Hall
HACKS

Priya
Krishna

Illustrations by Jude Buffum

Storey Publishing

The mission of Storey Publishing is to serve our customers by publishing practical information that encourages personal independence in harmony with the environment.

EDITED BY Margaret Sutherland
ART DIRECTION AND BOOK DESIGN BY
    Carolyn Eckert
TEXT PRODUCTION BY Liseann Karandisecky

ILLUSTRATIONS BY © Jude Buffum,
    except for pages 8–9, 23, 24, 37,
    38, 75, 90, 93, 101, 104, 118 and 119 by
    Carolyn Eckert
Author's photograph by Thea Stutsman

INDEXED BY Christine R. Lindemer, Boston
    Road Communications

© 2014 BY Priya Krishna

Storey Publishing
210 MASS MoCA Way
North Adams, MA 01247
www.storey.com

Printed in the United States by Versa Press
10 9 8 7 6 5 4 3 2 1

Library of Congress Cataloging-in-Publication Data

Krishna, Priya, 1991-
        Ultimate dining hall hacks / by Priya Krishna.
            pages cm
        Based on the column The DDS detective from
            the Dartmouth newspaper.
        Includes index.
        ISBN 978-1-61212-450-6 (pbk. : alk. paper)
        ISBN 978-1-61212-451-3 (ebook)
        1. Quick and easy cooking.
        2. College students—Nutrition.
        I. Title.
TX833.5.K83 2014
641.5'55—dc23

        2013045041

To Mom, Dad, and Meera,
for giving me the purest
and most unconditional love
and support, and to dear
old Dartmouth, whose people
and institutions have touched
and inspired me more
than they will ever know.

ACKNOWLEDGMENTS

Five years ago, I was sitting with my sister, Meera, at the Dartmouth student center having one of those classic freshman-year identity crises about what my niche would be in college. From that identity crisis came "The DDS Detective," the newspaper column that inspired this very book. So the first person I would like to thank is Meera, who gave me the confidence to carve out a path that had never been paved before. Meera, you challenge me to reach for the stars and pick me up when I'm down. You embody everything an older sister should be, and I don't tell you enough how much I look up to you. David, I know you were there at Collis too, so thanks.

Thank you to my mom; decades of watching you cook up memorable creations in our kitchen inspired a lot of the recipes in the pages of this cookbook. If Mom was the inspiration, Dad, or should I say Agent Krishna, you were the architect. I have no one but you to thank for helping with the nitty-gritty aspects of the cookbook — logistics is certainly the least fun part of writing a book, and this whole process would not have gone so smoothly without you. I appreciate everything you do for me on a daily basis.

Thank you to everyone at Storey Publishing for seeing something in my proposal and for being so open and receptive to my ideas throughout this entire process. I would like to give a sincere thank you to *The Dartmouth* newspaper, specifically Amita Kulkarni and Eve Ahearn for taking a chance on a naïve freshman's silly column idea. I want to give an enormous thanks to Dartmouth Dining Services, whose administrators have always been so supportive of me. I would particularly like to thank Don Reed for taking me to dining services conventions so I could gorge myself on samples and interview other food providers, and most important, for letting me test my recipes in the dining halls even after I had graduated.

Thank you to Gardiner Kreglow for tearing apart and subsequently helping me to rewrite my book proposal in Robinson Hall. Thea Stutsman, thank you for your wonderful photography work and for being such an excellent foodie partner-in-crime. Thank you to my roommates, Kate Taylor and Lauren Vespoli, for all of the moral support through the writing and publishing process and for throwing me the most amazing contract-signing party ever. Thank you to Kelly and the Tropin Family for giving me a place to finish writing in peace, even though you all think I am a food fetishist. Thank you, Pandora, and specifically the original Broadway cast of *Mamma Mia*. The songs of ABBA took on new meaning for me during the rough few weeks I spent finishing this manuscript.

Finally, thank you to all of my friends and family, for reading — or even just glancing at — "The DDS Detective," for enduring my long rants about food, and for helping me find the strength I never could have known I had to publish a book. Sometimes I feel like I am living in my own world and that what I find valuable and interesting is valuable and interesting to literally no one else, but you-all's support finally made me believe that I had something useful to say. You all gave me my voice. Thanks a million.

CONTENTS

 = 1 RECIPE

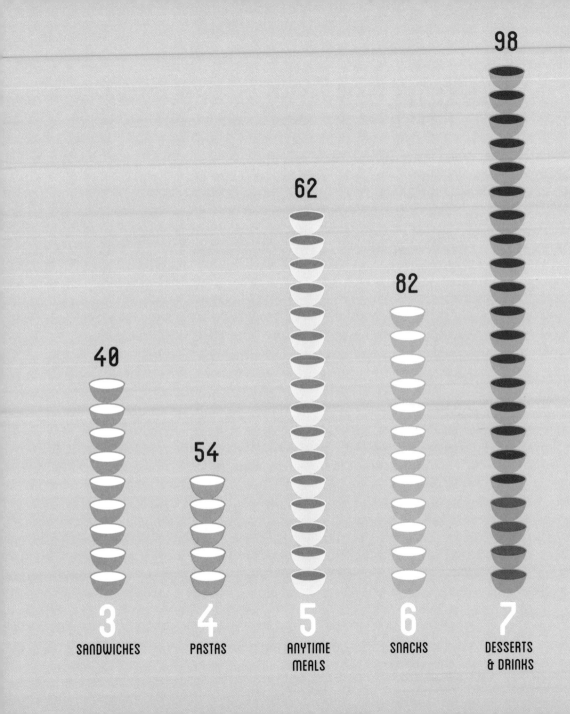

98

62

82

40

54

3
SANDWICHES

4
PASTAS

5
ANYTIME
MEALS

6
SNACKS

7
DESSERTS
& DRINKS

PREFACE

Going to college is an exciting yet terrifying experience.
There is the promise of starting fresh and exploring a world of possibilities.
But with turning over a new leaf comes the responsibility of being on your
own — and of feeding yourself. Whether you like it or not, eating is a central
part of the college experience. You make (and break) bonds over meals,
you fret about gaining the Freshman 15, and if you do freshman orientation
correctly, you attend only the events with free food. Food, to a large extent,
helps you figure out the direction you will take in college: the friends you
will make, the groups you will join, and the person you will be.

Maybe your parents will try — or have tried — to ease the transition to college by buying you "quick" and "easy" cookbooks and sending you care
packages every month in the hopes that food will be one less thing to worry
about. But then you get to college and encounter two big problems. First,
you don't have the time, money, or resources to cook. Between classes,
extracurricular activities, and making friends, it's hard to set aside time to
get ingredients and equipment (which all cost money), and to cook, eat,
and clean up. Your kitchen, if you have one, is laughable and could at best
aid you in microwaving a packet of Easy Mac.

A second and even larger problem has to do with the meal plan. Many
colleges mandate that students — particularly freshman — be on some
sort of meal plan, meaning that you feel obligated to eat your meals at
the dining halls because they are prepaid. But it is easy to get bored with

dining hall food and eventually resort to takeout most nights, effectively wasting the money you have already spent on a meal plan. And you can't survive on your parents' care packages forever. Does this situation sound familiar? If you haven't left for college yet, trust me; it will.

So when the realities of college dining inevitably start to unfold when you're on a meal plan, and you have zero time, will, and/or resources to cook, and you want to avoid getting stuck in a boring eating routine, that's where this cookbook comes in. The aim of these 75 recipes is to provide students like you with recipes that are easy to follow, easy to remember, and easy to customize on the fly. These recipes will allow you to transform the day-to-day items that most dining halls offer into dishes that you will not only enjoy, but find a lot more appealing than your standard cafeteria fare. Whether your dining hall is a state-of-the-art Google-esque situation or in a serious state of disrepair, you can use (and adapt) these recipes to make your meal plan a lot more exciting — even with limited resources. Armed with this book, you will never again view your meal plan as limiting and unappealing. You will be ready to face fearlessly any kind of dining hall and make delicious, varied meals at any time of the day.

I realize this idea is pretty out of the ordinary — shocking, even. So I have prepared a Q&A section to respond to any lingering doubts you might have about reading this cookbook.

Why are you qualified to write this cookbook? Can't anyone melt cheese on tortilla chips and call herself an author?

Put simply, while everyone else was joining a cappella groups and intramural softball teams during freshman orientation, I very confusingly decided to devote my entire extracurricular college experience to the dining halls. I wrote a weekly column in the newspaper in which I invented recipes that could be made with ingredients in the dining halls, and I worked as a consultant for the school's dining hall provider. Both gave me a wealth of knowledge about this cookbook's very subject matter. This may have looked lame to all the kids killing it on their sports teams, but I'm the one who got the book deal, and apparently my limited athleticism has finally paid off.

What if I have dietary restrictions, including but not limited to paleo, gluten-free, vegan, vegetarian, that new-wave Atkins diet, and pescatarian, and I also break out into hives when exposed to red-colored fruit?

In this book, the name of the game is flexibility. There are recipes for every diet and food preference out there, and each recipe is made to be customized. This isn't your traditional cookbook, with very specific directions, ingredients, or measurements. Instead, you should think of each recipe as a basic blueprint that you can alter based on your personal tastes. Each recipe also comes with suggestions for modifying the dish, so check out those if you are looking to change it up!

Will I be laughed at for doing something different with my food and not just getting the standard entrees available at the dining halls?

Um — no. Haven't you seen *21 Jump Street* (the movie starring Channing Tatum and Jonah Hill, obviously not the pre-2000s TV show)? Being more different-and-alternative Jonah Hill than jockish-and-mainstream Channing Tatum is totally cool now, so following these recipes is virtually guaranteed to boost your campus street cred.

I'm an on-the-go eater. Are these recipes takeout friendly?

Being a French major who wrote her thesis on why the true pleasures of dining involve spending hours at the table, I am obligated to tell you to take time out of your schedule to enjoy your meal and to avoid takeout. Being a former college student who had to balance school plus a million activities plus a social life, I get that from time to time, taking food to go may be necessary. That said, many of these recipes are very much to-go friendly and can probably be made right in a takeout container.

But every cafeteria is different! How can your recipes apply to any college dining hall?

Great question. Obviously I spent most of my time in the dining halls of my alma mater, but I also attended a few food services conventions while working as a dining hall consultant. At these conventions, I had the opportunity to talk to various schools' dining hall providers about the ingredients and equipment they usually had at their disposal. Combine that with a lot of Internet research and several field trips to visit friends at other colleges, and I ended up with quite a broad understanding of a lot of different kinds of dining halls. And as I mentioned before, not every dining hall will have every ingredient in this book, and that's okay — every recipe is designed to be adaptable.

This sounds like a lot of work. I think I'm just going to stick to takeout.

First of all, that's not a question. Second, every recipe takes about three minutes or less to make, which is considerably under the time it would take you to wait for the takeout person to come to your dorm. So trying these recipes can really only improve your eating situation.

Are these recipes healthy?

I define *healthy* as eating in a balanced way. These recipes aren't specifically designed to help you lose weight or anything like that, but I think they all fit nicely into a well-proportioned diet that includes whole ingredients and lots of different food groups. At the end of the day, the healthiest aspect of this cookbook is that each recipe forces you to be conscious of what ingredients you are putting into your body every day. People say this is the reason cooking for yourself, regardless of what you are cooking, is the healthiest way to eat — so think of this cookbook as a time- and resource-saving shortcut to healthful awareness.

I am not in college, and yet I have this cookbook in my possession. Can these recipes apply to me?

Yes! As a recent college graduate with budget constraints and a tiny kitchen, I can say with confidence that these recipes work just as well in the real world as they do in a dining hall. I haven't tried them within other institutions with limited dining options, but once I do, you can look out for my sequel, *Ultimate Jail Hacks: 75 Creative, Delicious Ways to Transform Prison Food and Make Your Fellow Inmates Jealous.*

Can't we just be done with the questions and get on with the cookbook already?

I thought you'd never ask! But first, turn the page for a quick guide on how best to use this cookbook.

How to Use This Cookbook

1. **These recipes are customizable and even include suggestions for modification.** I know I have said this a million times, but every dining hall is different, so utilize whatever resources you have. You don't have to run around your dining hall trying to use the exact ingredients specified in each recipe — make the recipes work for you, not the other way around.

2. **There are no measurements.** This is because, as you will see, this cookbook does not actually involve any real "cooking." Add as much or as little of an ingredient as your preferences dictate.

3. **Times are approximate.** All of the "cooking" times are based on the equipment I used to test the recipes. Your microwave, for example, may be a lot stronger than mine, requiring you to adapt the recipes slightly. I trust that you can figure it out — after all, you did get into college.

4. **If a recipe doesn't seem to-go friendly to you, you can make it that way.** One easy way is to put the ingredients in a wrap (Eggs Carbonara becomes a delicious breakfast burrito, for example) or press them in a panini press. Disposable soup bowls or your own reusable bowls with lids are also convenient. Many are microwave friendly, and you can make practically anything in them.

7. **Assume serving sizes of one for each recipe.** That means: for bread, I usually mean one or two slices, and for meats, I mean enough to feed one (e.g., one chicken breast). I am assuming here that you are not planning on throwing dinner parties at the dining hall, but if you are, please send me photos.

5. **I developed these recipes to satisfy my tastes and preferences, but they only scratch the surface of the possibilities in your dining hall.** My overall hope is that this book inspires you to make your own creations in the dining hall based on the ingredients that you love the most.

8. When you see **PYOP**, this means "Pick Your Own Protein," as in, choose whatever protein you like best, be it chicken, steak, pork, tofu, or anything else.

6. **Don't forget about microwave safety.** Don't be that person who put a steel plate in the microwave and started a cafeteria fire, and more important, remember that dishes may be hot when you take them out of the microwave. It is better to be safe than sorry and use two napkins as makeshift oven mitts when removing plates that have been in the microwave longer than a minute.

List of Ingredients & Equipment

This is an exhaustive list of all the potential ingredients and equipment you might need for this cookbook. This is not to say that if you don't have all of these ingredients and equipment you cannot use this book — the list is just to give you an idea of many of the items you are most likely to find in your average dining hall. If you don't have something, there will always be alternatives.

FRUITS AND VEGETABLES

- Apples
- Artichokes
- Avocado
- Bananas
- Bean sprouts
- Bell peppers
- Broccoli
- Carrots
- Corn
- Cucumbers
- Lemon
- Mangoes
- Mushrooms
- Olives
- Onions
- Peaches
- Peas
- Pineapple
- Potatoes (and also French fries)
- Raisins
- Salad greens (kale, lettuce, and spinach)
- Tomatoes
- Spinach
- Strawberries
- Sweet potatoes
- Vegetable soup

GRAINS

- Bagels
- Bread
- Cereal
- Croutons
- Granola
- Hamburger bun
- Oatmeal
- Pasta
- Pita
- Pizza
- Rice
- Tortillas & tortilla chips
- Waffles

DAIRY

- Butter
- Cheddar cheese
- Cottage cheese
- Cream cheese
- Eggs
- Feta
- Milk (or soy milk)
- Mozzarella
- Parmesan cheese
- Whipped cream
- Yogurt

DRINKS

- Coffee
- Hot chocolate powder
- Juice
- Soda
- Tea

EQUIPMENT

- Blender
- Ice machine
- Microwave
- Panini press
- Sauté or grill bar
- Toaster
- Waffle maker

SAUCES AND OTHER CONDIMENTS AND SEASONINGS

- Alfredo sauce
- Balsamic vinegar
- Barbecue sauce
- Chili sauce
- Garlic *(typically either garlic oil or garlic powder)*
- Guacamole
- Honey
- Hot sauce
- Hummus
- Jalapenos
- Jam
- Ketchup
- Maple syrup
- Mustard
- Olive oil
- Peanut butter
- Pesto
- Salsa
- Soy sauce
- Teriyaki sauce *(or any other kind of Asian sauce)*

PROTEINS

- Bacon
- Beans
- Chicken
- Fish
- Hamburger patty
- Meatballs
- Pepperoni or salami
- Tofu
- Any other protein of your preference

SWEETS

- Brownies
- Cake
- Chocolate *(either candies or chocolate chips)*
- Cookies
- Graham crackers
- Ice cream
- Marshmallows
- Shredded sweetened coconut
- Sugar

HERBS AND SPICES

- Chili powder
- Cinnamon
- Crushed red pepper flakes
- Oregano
- Salt and pepper

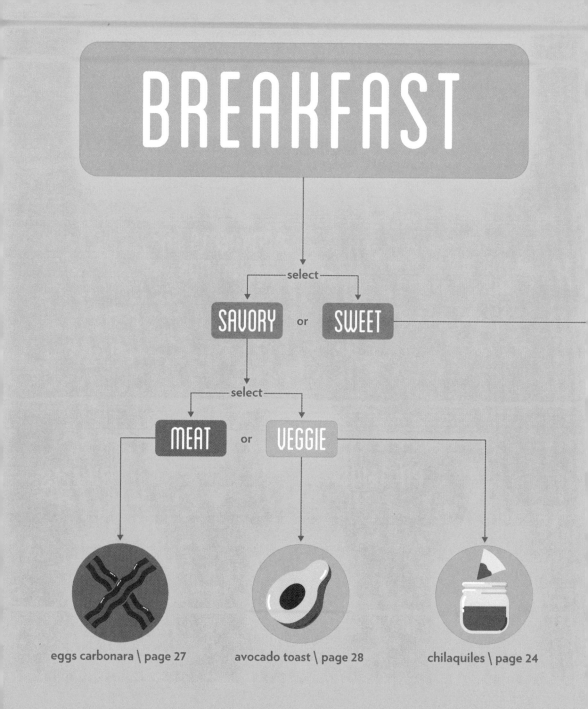

BREAKFAST

select

SAVORY or SWEET

select

MEAT or VEGGIE

eggs carbonara \ page 27

avocado toast \ page 28

chilaquiles \ page 24

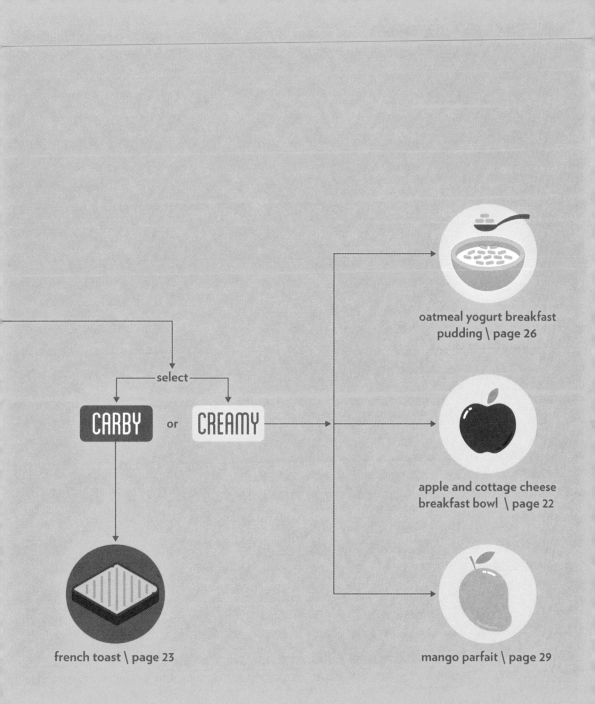

oatmeal yogurt breakfast
pudding \ page 26

select

CARBY or CREAMY

apple and cottage cheese
breakfast bowl \ page 22

french toast \ page 23

mango parfait \ page 29

Apple and Cottage Cheese Breakfast Bowl

I had never tried cottage cheese before coming to college and was frankly a little scared by it, but I now realize that it is a total sleeper hit as a breakfast item. In a lot of typical dishes that call for yogurt, you can use cottage cheese to make them a lot more filling — like this recipe, which pairs cottage cheese with lemon- and cinnamon-coated fruit for a really hearty start to the day.

INGREDIENTS

>> Bowl of apple slices
(I also love using strawberries.)

>> Brown sugar

>> Cinnamon

>> Lemon wedges

>> Cottage cheese

EQUIPMENT

>> Microwave, *optional*

1. **Coat the apple slices** with a heaping spoonful of brown sugar and a shake or two of cinnamon.

2. **Squeeze a little lemon juice over the apples.** If you'd like, microwave the apples for about 1 minute to warm the fruit and melt the sugar.

3. **In a separate bowl,** mix a little more brown sugar into some cottage cheese. Add the apple mixture to the cottage cheese, and stir it all together.

French Toast

French toast is sometimes overshadowed in the brunch department by its more popular cousins, the pancake and the egg. But as a dish, it has so much to offer: cinnamon and syrup-soaked bread with fresh fruit and melting butter on top — the perfect lazy Sunday breakfast.

INGREDIENTS

- Egg
- Milk or vanilla soy milk
- Sugar
- Cinnamon, *optional*
- Thick piece of white bread
- Butter
- Honey or maple syrup
- Strawberries, chopped

EQUIPMENT

- Toaster
- Microwave

1. **Crack the egg into a bowl** and beat it with a fork. Mix in a few big spoonfuls of milk or soy milk and a few shakes of sugar, and cinnamon, if you'd like.

2. **Lightly toast the bread,** then soak it in the egg mixture for a minute or so.

3. **Microwave the bread** on high for 1 minute on each side, or until the egg has cooked into the bread.

4. **Spread butter** on top of the piece of French toast. Drizzle honey or maple syrup and add chopped strawberries on top.

RAW EGGS
Most dining halls will not have plain eggs out for the taking, but it's easy to ask for one wherever you see eggs being served.

Chilaquiles

Chilaquiles are a super flavorful Mexican breakfast dish made of tortillas and eggs. I had this meal for the first time when I attended summer camp in Cuernavaca, Mexico, during high school. If you are into breakfast burritos or huevos rancheros, you should definitely consider adding chilaquiles to your morning routine.

INGREDIENTS

» Tortillas or tortilla chips
» Tomato sauce
» Salsa
» Grated cheddar cheese
» Beans
» Scrambled eggs
» Avocado, *optional*

EQUIPMENT

» Microwave

TORTILLAS VS. TORTILLA CHIPS
Use tortillas if you want your chilaquiles to taste more enchilada-esque, and tortilla chips if you want a little extra crunch in each bite.

1. **Rip the tortillas** into bite-size pieces and spread them out on a plate. If using tortilla chips, just put a big handful on a plate.

2. **Pour a large scoop** each of tomato sauce and salsa over the tortillas.

3. **Add grated cheese, beans, and eggs,** and microwave the dish for 1 minute, or until the cheese melts.

4. **Top with avocado slices** and more cheese, if you'd like.

Oatmeal Yogurt Breakfast Pudding

I discovered this combination while I was studying abroad in London, and I think I ate it almost every single day for breakfast. If you aspire to fall into a similar routine, I definitely suggest changing it up with different kinds of sweeteners, fruits, and yogurts to avoid repetitiveness.

INGREDIENTS

>> Bowl of oatmeal
>> Yogurt *(I prefer plain, vanilla, or strawberry.)*
>> Banana
>> Honey

1. **Let the oatmeal cool down** for a minute, or longer, depending on how hot it is.

2. **Slowly stir the yogurt** into the oatmeal.

3. **Slice the banana into the bowl** and mix it into the oatmeal and yogurt. Top with a drizzle of honey.

Eggs Carbonara

Carbonara is traditionally associated with dinner, but its main components — eggs, bacon, Parmesan cheese, and pepper — work even better as a simple breakfast dish. These eggs can make a quick transition to lunch or dinner, though — just add pasta!

INGREDIENTS

>> Bacon
>> Plate of over-easy eggs *(Other egg preparations work, too.)*
>> Olive oil
>> Parmesan cheese
>> Pepper

1. Crumble a few bacon strips into pieces over the eggs. Drizzle olive oil on top.

2. Finish with a sprinkling of Parmesan and a healthy dusting of pepper, freshly ground if possible.

Avocado Toast

When my mother can't decide what to make for breakfast when I am at home, she spreads half of an avocado on a piece of toast and tops it with our secret family spice. While I can almost guarantee that your dining hall does not stock the Krishna spice blend, you can top a piece of avocado toast with virtually anything (barring a few exceptions) to make a super-satisfying breakfast.

INGREDIENTS
» Your favorite toasting bread
» Avocado
» Salt and pepper
» Toppings of your choice *(My favorites include crushed red pepper, Parmesan cheese, salsa, olive oil, pesto, or a fried egg.)*

EQUIPMENT
» Toaster

1. Toast the bread.

2. Mash about half of an avocado onto the toast and sprinkle salt and pepper on top.

3. Add more toppings to suit your mood.

Mango Parfait

Mangoes and cinnamon make this dish a little more interesting than your everyday granola parfait, and it is always my go-to as a healthy breakfast or post-workout snack.

INGREDIENTS
- Cup of mango chunks or slices
- Plain yogurt
- Granola
- Cinnamon
- Honey

1. **Add a scoop of plain yogurt** to your cup of mango pieces.

2. **Top with a small handful of granola,** a few shakes of cinnamon, and a drizzle of honey.

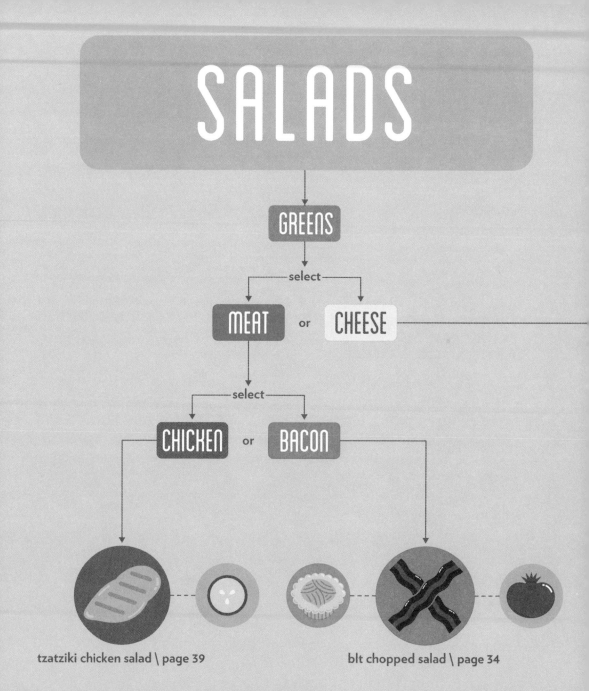

SALADS

GREENS

select

MEAT or CHEESE

select

CHICKEN or BACON

tzatziki chicken salad \ page 39

blt chopped salad \ page 34

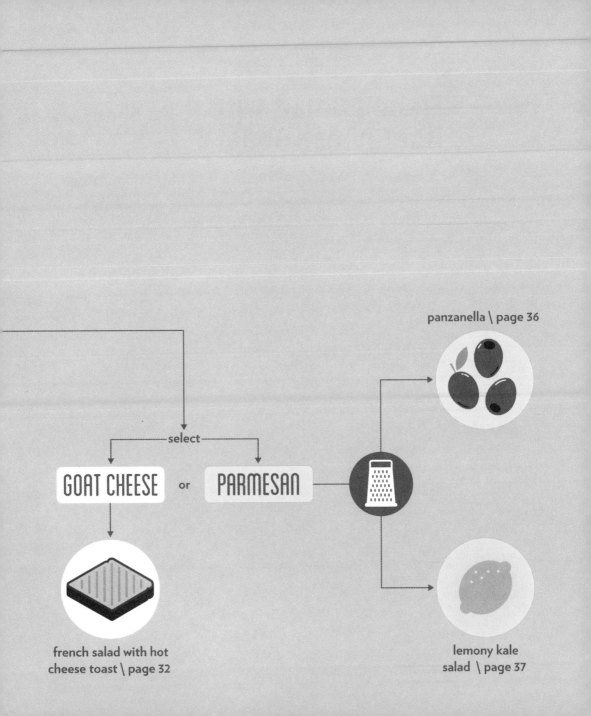

panzanella \ page 36

select

GOAT CHEESE or PARMESAN

french salad with hot
cheese toast \ page 32

lemony kale
salad \ page 37

French Salad with Hot Cheese Toast

This recipe is inspired by a dish my host family would often make for me when I was studying abroad in Toulouse, France. The French name for this dish is "Salade au Chèvre Chaud" which translates to "Salad with Hot Goat Cheese."

It is pretty safe to imagine that putting a melted-cheese toast on plain greens would make them taste a lot better, but the real star here is the honey, which adds the perfect touch of sweetness.

INGREDIENTS
» Thick piece of bread
» Goat cheese, cream cheese, or Swiss cheese
» Mustard
» Olive oil
» Balsamic vinegar
» Brown sugar
» Plate of salad greens
» Honey

EQUIPMENT
» Toaster, *optional*
» Microwave, *optional*

1. **Toast a piece of bread** or simply use a good, sturdy untoasted slice.

2. **Spread the cheese on top.** If you are using a non-spreadable cheese, microwave the bread with the cheese on top until the cheese melts.

3. **Mix together equal parts mustard, olive oil, balsamic vinegar,** and a pinch of brown sugar in a cup and then pour the dressing over your greens.

4. **Toss the salad** to distribute the dressing.

5. **Place the cheese toast on top** of the salad, and drizzle honey over the entire dish.

**SIMPLE
VINAIGRETTE**
Skip the
bottled,
preservative-
laden dress-
ings at the
salad
bar and make
your own.
It is as easy
as choosing
your favorite
combination
of oil, vinegar,
lemon, herbs,
and spices.
Give every-
thing a quick
stir in a cup,
and it's ready
to dress any
salad.

BLT Chopped Salad

You won't find many actual salad recipes in this cookbook because I generally don't find them very satisfying as a meal. This one, however, is loaded with bacon, feta, corn, and avocado — ingredients that are packed with flavor and also really filling.

INGREDIENTS

» Bowl of lettuce
» Tomato
» Avocado
» Corn
» Feta cheese

» Bacon *(Please do not use bacon bits here. They are gross.)*
» Olive oil
» Lemon wedges
» Salt and pepper

1. **Prepare the salad** by adding tomato, avocado, corn, and feta to your lettuce.

2. **Crumble a strip of bacon** over the top of the salad.

3. **Make the dressing** by mixing olive oil, lemon juice, salt, and pepper in a cup or small bowl, and then pour it over the salad.

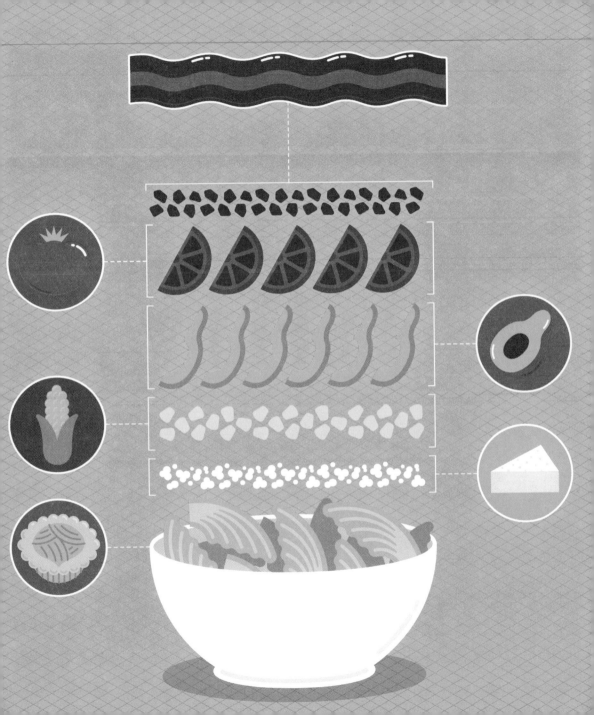

Panzanella

If Ina Garten (aka The Barefoot Contessa — one of my culinary idols) were a food, I imagine she would be Panzanella, an Italian bread salad, because it is a classy, composed, rustic yet commanding dish with serious flavor. Each bite is bursting with the juices from the oil-and-vinegar-soaked pieces of bread.

INGREDIENTS

» Your favorite bread
» Tomato
» Onions
» Olives
» Bell peppers

» Olive oil
» Balsamic vinegar
» Parmesan cheese
» Salt and pepper

1. **Break the bread into pieces** in a bowl. Add the tomato, onions, olives, and peppers.

2. **Dress the salad** with olive oil and balsamic vinegar, and mix so that all the bread pieces and vegetables are nicely coated with the dressing.

3. **Finish with a sprinkle** of Parmesan, pepper, and a little salt.

Lemony Kale Salad

Before all you kale skeptics turn the page — I promise this salad will be a revelation. Kale is hitting dining halls everywhere, and perhaps it's time you got on board with this new-wave leafy green. This recipe mellows the otherwise strong vegetal taste of kale with lemon, cheese, and croutons. Case in point: it is the only kale dish my kale-hating friend, Eliza, will eat.

INGREDIENTS

>> Olive oil
>> Lemon wedges
>> Croutons
>> Raw kale
>> Parmesan cheese

1. **Make the dressing** by combining the olive oil and a little lemon juice in a bowl. Toss in a generous handful of crumbled croutons and stir.

2. **Mix the dressing** into the kale; toss well.

3. **Sprinkle the top** with Parmesan.

TENDER KALE

An odd but great tip to give your kale a silkier, more palatable texture: try rubbing the leaves together before dressing. Some call this massaging your kale, and I find that pretty strange — but I promise, it actually works!

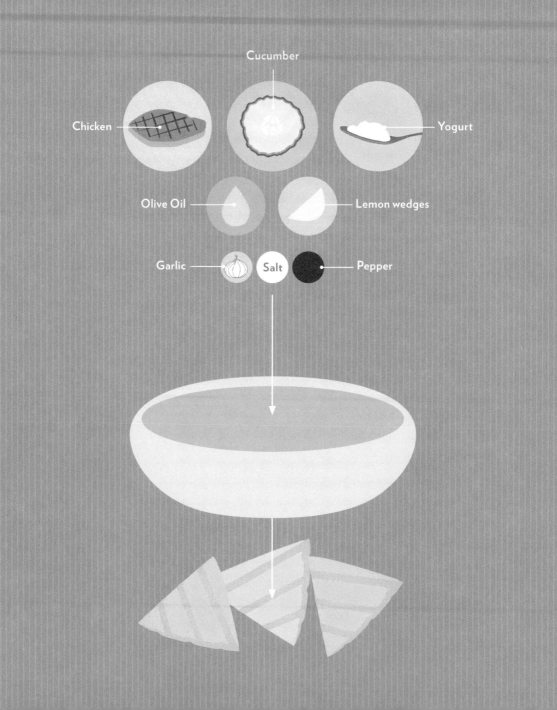

Chicken

Cucumber

Yogurt

Olive Oil

Lemon wedges

Garlic

Salt

Pepper

Tzatziki Chicken Salad

Tzatziki is a constant reminder for me of how perfect and versatile a food plain yogurt is. A common way to eat yogurt is to mix in some granola and fruit and eat it as a snack or as breakfast. But if you add a little garlic, olive oil, and lemon, it becomes a refreshing, savory sauce that makes for a healthier, Mediterranean take on traditional chicken salad.

INGREDIENTS

» Grilled chicken
» Cucumber
» Plain yogurt (preferably Greek)
» Olive oil
» Lemon wedges

» Garlic oil or garlic powder
» Salt and pepper
» Bread, pita, or chips, optional

1. **Cut chicken and cucumber into bite-size pieces** and put into a bowl.

2. **Add a few spoonfuls of yogurt** and toss the ingredients. The chicken should be thoroughly coated by but not drowning in the yogurt.

3. **Stir in a little bit of olive oil** and squeeze in the juice of one to two lemon wedges.

4. **Add** garlic, salt, and pepper.

5. **Enjoy on a sandwich,** in a pita, with chips, or by itself.

SANDWICHES

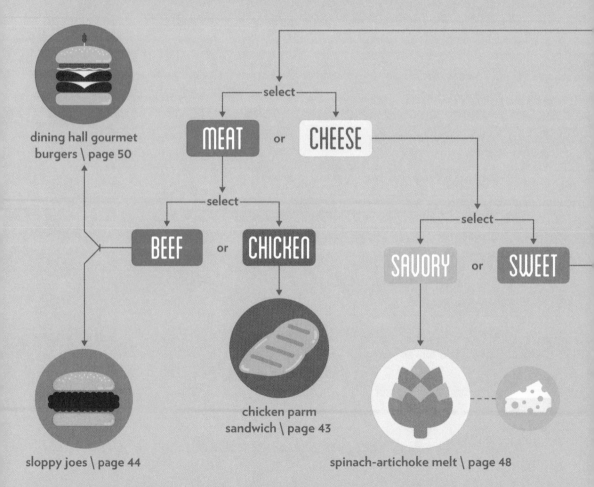

dining hall gourmet
burgers \ page 50

select

MEAT or CHEESE

select

BEEF or CHICKEN

select

SAVORY or SWEET

chicken parm
sandwich \ page 43

sloppy joes \ page 44

spinach-artichoke melt \ page 48

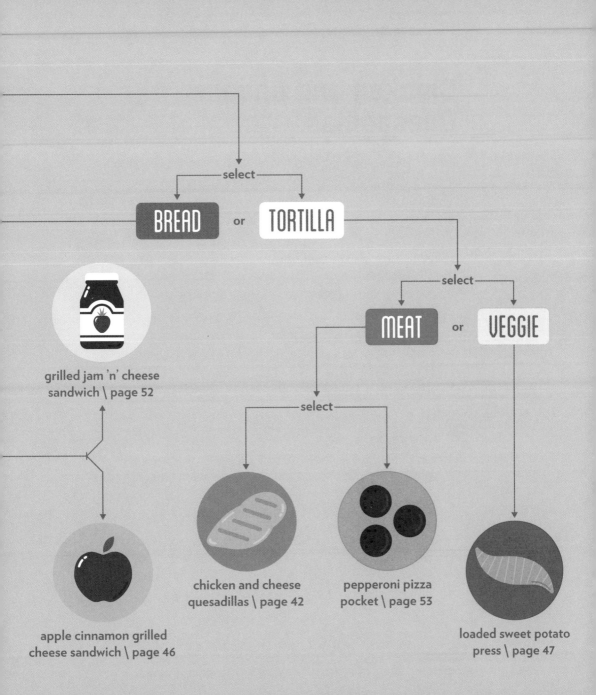

select

BREAD or **TORTILLA**

select

MEAT or **VEGGIE**

select

grilled jam 'n' cheese
sandwich \ page 52

select

chicken and cheese
quesadillas \ page 42

pepperoni pizza
pocket \ page 53

apple cinnamon grilled
cheese sandwich \ page 46

loaded sweet potato
press \ page 47

Chicken and Cheese Quesadillas

When I was younger, I would make these quesadillas whenever I was really hungry after school and dinner wasn't ready yet. Good news: you can make quesadillas in a dining hall when you are just as desperate for something quick and basic. Try experimenting with different types of fillings. I like adding pesto or roasted red peppers.

INGREDIENTS

» Sliced grilled chicken
» Grated cheese
   (I recommend cheddar.)
» Tortilla
» Toppings of your choice, including salsa, guacamole and, sour cream

EQUIPMENT

» Panini press or microwave

1. Arrange the chicken and cheese on one side of the tortilla.

2. Fold the tortilla over and press in a panini press until you see dark grill marks. If you don't have a panini press, microwave the quesadilla for about 1 minute, or until the cheese is fully melted.

3. Cut into pieces and enjoy with your favorite toppings.

Chicken Parm Sandwich

Sticking chicken Parmesan between two pieces of bread may seem a little too decadent, a little too reminiscent of something Paula Deen might make, but it totally works with this sandwich. Grilled chicken topped with gooey cheese and rich tomato sauce, all between crusty bread slices, makes for the ideal bite. Skip the second slice of bread and have it open-faced if you're looking for something a little less substantial.

INGREDIENTS

>> Plate of grilled chicken
(Grilled eggplant works well too.)

>> Tomato sauce

>> Parmesan cheese

>> Bread *(the crustier the better)*

EQUIPMENT

>> Microwave

>> Toaster

1. **Top the chicken** with tomato sauce and cheese.

2. **Microwave the whole dish** for about 40 seconds, or until the cheese melts.

3. **Toast two pieces of bread.**

4. **Place the chicken Parmesan** between the two slices of bread to make a sandwich.

Sloppy Joes

I first learned what Sloppy Joes were when I watched the under-appreciated Mary-Kate and Ashley movie *It Takes Two* and Mary-Kate (or Ashley?) called them "big, gooey, messy burgers." I can guarantee that this Sloppy Joe, which is loaded with plenty of meat and spicy tomato flavor, lives up to both of its names. Make sure you aren't wearing white when you make this one!

INGREDIENTS
>> Meatball
>> Tomato sauce
>> Ketchup
>> Hot sauce, such as Tabasco
>> Chili powder
>> Hamburger bun
   (toasted, if you want your Sloppy Joe to be less sloppy)

1. **Top a meatball** with a few big spoonfuls of tomato sauce, a generous squirt of ketchup, hot sauce, and a dash of chili powder.

2. **Use a fork to mash** the meatball.

3. **Spoon the meat** into the hamburger bun.

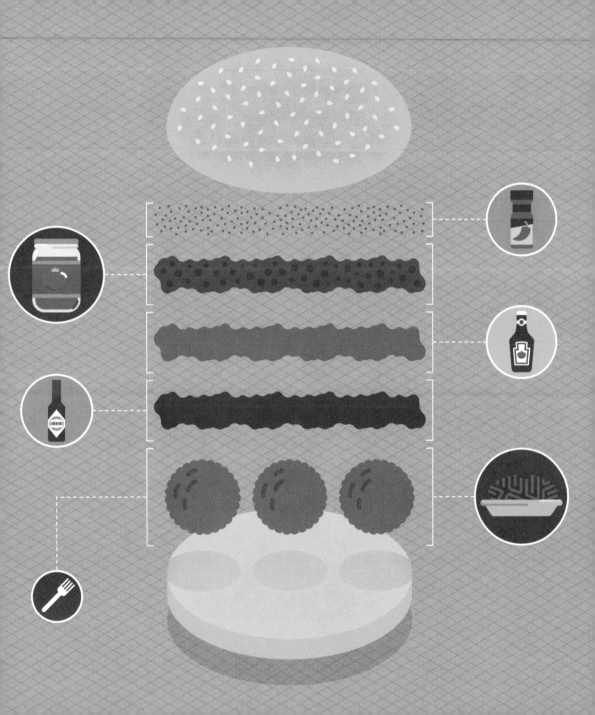

Apple Cinnamon Grilled Cheese Sandwich*

Even the biggest grilled cheese purists like myself can get behind this sandwich. The cinnamon-sugar caramelizes in the panini press, and the apples "bake" to golden perfection. Alongside nutty cheddar cheese, it is a match made in heaven.

INGREDIENTS

>> Sliced apples
   (the thinner the better)
>> Cinnamon
>> Brown sugar
>> Bread
>> Cheddar cheese

EQUIPMENT

>> Panini press

1. **Toss apple slices in equal parts** cinnamon and brown sugar.

2. **Cover one slice of bread** with cheddar cheese.

3. **Stack the apples** on the other slice of bread.

4. **Close the sandwich and press it** in a panini press until the cheese has melted.

* See cover illustration.

Loaded Sweet Potato Press

Sweet potatoes are another one of those ingredients that can work in practically endless ways. They are perfect in a recipe like this because the soft flesh is easy to spread on a tortilla and their natural sweetness goes really well with salsa and cheese. Add chili powder if you are looking to kick it up a notch.

INGREDIENTS

» Sweet potato *(or a regular potato if you can mash it)*
» Tortilla
» Salsa
» Black beans
» Cheese
» Rice

EQUIPMENT

» Panini press, *optional*

1. **Spoon the potato** out of the skin and spread it onto one side of the tortilla.

2. **Mix a little bit of salsa** into the potato.

3. **Top the potato** with black beans, cheese, and rice.

4. **Fold the tortilla in half,** and grill in the panini press, or roll it up and eat it burrito style.

Spinach-Artichoke Melt

I know many people who hate spinach and artichokes but love spinach-artichoke dip because it has so many crave-worthy characteristics: it's gooey, hot, melty, and really cheesy. The only way to make this dip even better is to make it portable by putting it between two slices of bread.

INGREDIENTS

» Cream cheese
» Bread
» Garlic powder
» Fresh spinach
» Swiss or mozzarella cheese

» Artichokes
(*plain canned or marinated*)
» Salt and pepper

EQUIPMENT

» Panini press

1. Spread cream cheese on one slice of bread and sprinkle garlic powder on top.

2. Stack the spinach, cheese, and artichokes on top of the cream cheese.

3. Add a few shakes of salt and pepper.

4. Put another slice of bread on top and press the sandwich in the panini press until you see dark grill marks and all the cheese has melted.

DINING HALL GOURMET BURGERS

Hamburgers are one of the most standard dining hall offerings, but with a few added ingredients, you can make yours a lot more interesting. This section will provide a few ideas to help make your burger extra special.

Start with a regular hamburger (bun + patty), and add . . .

TEX-MEX BURGER

Salsa

Cheddar cheese

Crushed tortilla chips

CHILI BURGER

Cheddar cheese

Chili

Bacon

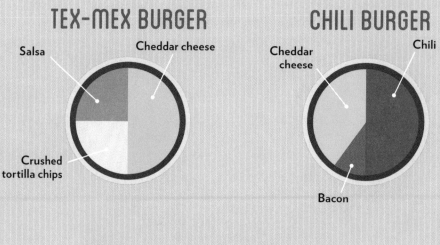

= HAMBURGER & BUN FROM ABOVE

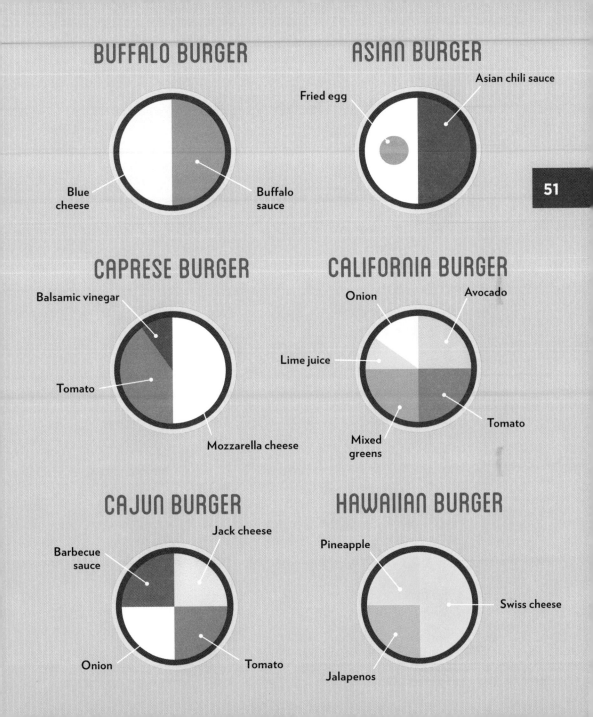

BUFFALO BURGER

Blue cheese
Buffalo sauce

ASIAN BURGER

Fried egg
Asian chili sauce

CAPRESE BURGER

Balsamic vinegar
Tomato
Mozzarella cheese

CALIFORNIA BURGER

Onion
Avocado
Lime juice
Tomato
Mixed greens

CAJUN BURGER

Jack cheese
Barbecue sauce
Onion
Tomato

HAWAIIAN BURGER

Pineapple
Swiss cheese
Jalapenos

Grilled Jam 'n' Cheese Sandwich

Think grilled cheese sandwich meets strawberry shortcake. Jam and cream cheese are two of my favorite condiments, and they taste even better together in this sandwich.

INGREDIENTS
- » Cream cheese
- » Bread
- » Strawberry jam
- » Butter

EQUIPMENT
- » Panini press

1. **Spread cream cheese** on one piece of bread and strawberry jam on a second slice.

2. **Close the sandwich and swipe a little butter** on the outside of both pieces of bread.

3. **Grill in a panini press** just until the butter has melted and the sandwich is golden.

DESSERT PANINIS

Panini presses can deliver excellent desserts. Another favorite of mine is the S'mores Panini, which you can make with hot fudge or Nutella and mini marshmallows.

Pepperoni Pizza Pocket

This is essentially a much better (and healthier) version of a Hot Pocket, a fixture of many students' college experience. I like using different kinds of cheeses and salami instead of pepperoni to make the pizza pocket a little more interesting.

INGREDIENTS
- » Tomato sauce
- » Tortilla
- » Pepperoni or salami
- » Cheese *(I prefer mozzarella or cheddar.)*
- » Oregano

EQUIPMENT
- » Panini press or microwave

1. **Spread tomato sauce** down the center of the tortilla.

2. **Top with pepperoni or salami,** cheese, and a few shakes of oregano.

3. **Roll up like a burrito,** tucking in the sides, and grill in a panini press or heat in a microwave until the cheese is melted.

PASTAS

select

NO DAIRY or **CHEESE**

select

FISH or **NO MEAT**

teriyaki pasta \ page 58

alfredo salmon spaghetti \ page 60

mac and cheese \ page 56

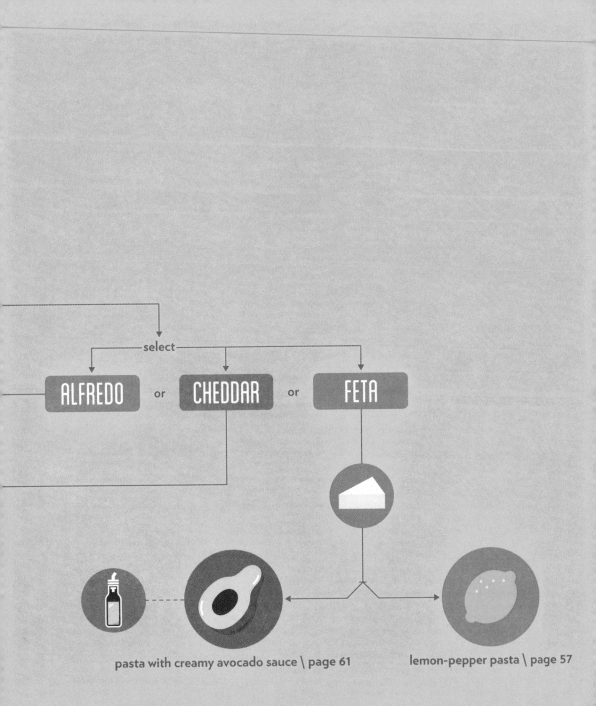

select

ALFREDO or CHEDDAR or FETA

pasta with creamy avocado sauce \ page 61

lemon-pepper pasta \ page 57

Mac and Cheese

I firmly believe that it is almost impossible to screw up a dish that consists of cheese and pasta, so instead of messing around with a classic, I decided to do mac and cheese the way I know best: creamy pasta with a super-crunchy crumb crust on top.

INGREDIENTS
>> Alfredo sauce or butter
>> Bowl of pasta *(preferably of the elbow variety)*
>> Parmesan cheese
>> Cheddar cheese
>> Croutons

EQUIPMENT
>> Microwave

1. **Mix Alfredo sauce into the pasta.** If you don't have Alfredo sauce, you can use plain butter; just be sure to soften it in the microwave before mixing it into the pasta.

2. **Sprinkle a layer** of Parmesan and a layer of cheddar cheese on top of the pasta.

3. **Crush about two handfuls of croutons** into crumbs in a bowl and sprinkle them on top of the pasta.

4. **Microwave the dish** until the cheese melts and the crouton crumbs settle into the pasta — about 1 minute.

Lemon-Pepper Pasta

Lemon-pepper pasta is one of those dishes that I made constantly in my college dining hall and continue to make in my New York apartment because it is so simple, yet somehow tastes really fancy. Use cracked pepper in this recipe if you have it — it elevates the whole dish.

INGREDIENTS

» Olive oil
» Lemon wedges
» Bowl of pasta
» Garlic powder
» Salt and pepper
» Parmesan or feta cheese

1. Drizzle olive oil and the juice from a few lemon wedges over the pasta and toss to coat.

2. Mix in garlic powder, salt, and plenty of pepper.

3. Top with cheese.

Teriyaki Pasta

Stir-fry obviously tastes great over rice, but it tastes even better over pasta because most kinds of pasta are made to absorb sauces. I love using Teriyaki sauce, but you can mix and match with your favorite flavors, or just keep it simple with soy sauce.

INGREDIENTS

» Bowl of pasta
» Teriyaki sauce
» PYOP *(pick your own protein)*
» Vegetables of your choice *(I prefer red peppers, broccoli, and carrots.)*
» Lime, *optional*
» Chili sauce, *optional*

EQUIPMENT

» Microwave or sauté bar

1. **Add teriyaki sauce, your protein pick, and vegetables** to the pasta and either toss the pasta at a sauté bar or microwave for about 2 minutes.

2. **Top with a squeeze** of lime juice and/or chili sauce, if you'd like.

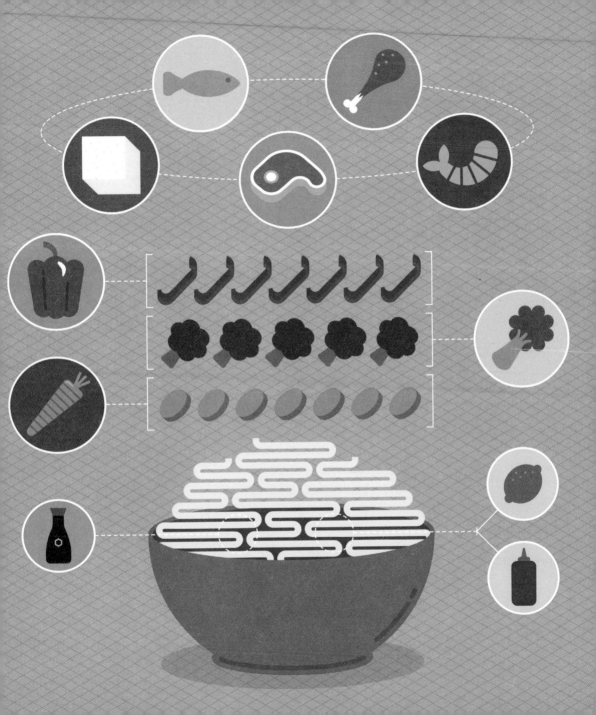

Alfredo Salmon Spaghetti

This dish is another one of my French host family's greatest hits from my study-abroad term. The Alfredo sauce becomes infused with salmon flavor, and the whole thing tastes kind of like a salmon carbonara.

INGREDIENTS
» Salmon fillet
» Bowl of pasta *(I prefer to use spaghetti here, but any kind works.)*
» Alfredo sauce
» Salt and pepper

1. Flake the salmon fillet into the spaghetti.

2. Add a scoop of Alfredo sauce and gently mix the salmon and sauce with the pasta.

3. Season the dish with a few shakes of salt and pepper.

Pasta with Creamy Avocado Sauce

I have seen many variations of avocado pasta sauce on vegan cooking blogs, so naturally I decided to add cheese to my version. The result is a silky, tangy sauce that will mix up your pasta routine.

INGREDIENTS

>> Avocados or avocado spread
>> Olive oil
>> Feta cheese
>> Garlic powder
>> Lemon wedges
>> Salt and pepper
>> Pasta

1. **Mash the avocado in a bowl,** and then mix in olive oil, crumbled feta, a little bit of garlic powder, and lemon juice. Season with salt and pepper.

2. **Toss the pasta in the sauce,** and add a little more feta and olive oil on top.

ANYTIME MEALS

select

PYOP CHICKEN or VEGGIE

enchiladas \ page 65

select

balsamic caprese chicken \ page 76

satay \ page 74 chicken and waffles \ page 71 chicken pot pie \ page 81

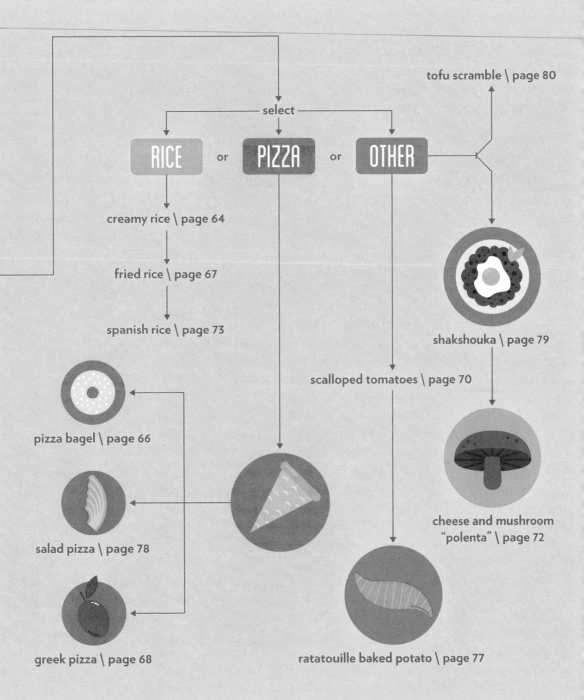

select

RICE or PIZZA or OTHER

tofu scramble \ page 80

creamy rice \ page 64

fried rice \ page 67

spanish rice \ page 73

shakshouka \ page 79

scalloped tomatoes \ page 70

pizza bagel \ page 66

salad pizza \ page 78

cheese and mushroom "polenta" \ page 72

greek pizza \ page 68

ratatouille baked potato \ page 77

Creamy Rice

No matter what anyone tries to tell you, a cup of soup (particularly one of the non-cream-based variety) is not a meal. It is a snack or an appetizer, at best. However, mix your favorite bean or vegetable soup with rice and yogurt, and it all of a sudden becomes pretty hearty, not to mention (as the name suggests) really creamy.

INGREDIENTS

» Bowl of any kind of non-cream-based soup
   (preferably bean/vegetable soups)
» Rice
» Plain yogurt

1. **Mix equal parts soup and rice** together (the rice should not be drowning in the soup).

2. **Add a few dollops of yogurt,** and mix to incorporate.
   Make sure not to add so much that the yogurt overwhelms the flavor of the soup — less is more in this case!

A TIP ABOUT TEMPERATURE
Adding the yogurt does cool down this dish, but it's delicious eaten at around room temperature. If you want to keep it super hot, though, heat up the soup and rice a little more in the microwave before adding in the yogurt.

Enchiladas

I'm from Texas, so few things make me happier than Tex-Mex cuisine, and even fewer things make me happier than a plate of enchiladas. The trick with this dining hall version is to coat your tortillas with plenty of salsa to keep the enchiladas nice and juicy.

INGREDIENTS
» Corn or flour tortillas
» Salsa
» Grated cheddar cheese
» PYOP (pick your own protein)
» Sour cream, optional

EQUIPMENT
» Microwave

1. Generously coat one side of each tortilla with salsa. Layer cheese and your protein pick on top of the salsa and roll it up into a burrito.

2. Top the dish with a generous amount of salsa and more cheese.

3. Microwave the enchiladas for about 2 minutes.

4. Top the final product with a bit of sour cream, if you'd like.

Pizza Bagel

When I was little, my mother started making me pizza bagels so that I would stop pestering her to buy me Bagel Bites, and I still love them. When normal late-night fare like mozzarella sticks or grilled cheese sandwiches just isn't cutting it, pizza bagels are an excellent midnight snack.

INGREDIENTS
» Plain bagel
» Tomato sauce
» Cheese *(Mozzarella and cheddar work great.)*

EQUIPMENT
» Toaster
» Microwave

1. **Cut the bagel in half** and toast both halves.

2. **Top each half** with tomato sauce and grated cheese.

3. **Microwave the bagel halves for about 1 minute,** until the cheese melts.

Fried Rice

Fried rice is one of my favorite hibachi staples. This recipe may not get you all the live theatrics, but it is really easy to make and captures the same fantastic flavors. Feel free to nix the egg if it's not your thing.

INGREDIENTS
>> Bowl of rice
>> Peas
>> Corn
>> Salad oil
>> Soy sauce
>> Scrambled eggs, *optional*

EQUIPMENT
>> Microwave or sauté bar

1. **Mix peas, corn, oil, and soy sauce into the rice.** Add a small scoop of scrambled eggs, if you'd like.

2. **Microwave for about 1 minute,** or cook it at a sauté bar.

Greek Pizza

It's pizza — Greek-ified. Swap out tomato sauce for hummus and mozzarella for feta, load on the olives, tomatoes, and cucumber, put it all on top of a grilled pita, and you've got yourself a great alternative to your everyday slice of pizza.

INGREDIENTS
>> Pita
>> Hummus
>> Feta cheese
>> Olives
>> Cucumber
>> Tomato
>> Olive oil

EQUIPMENT
>> Panini press

1. Grill the pita in the panini press until you start to see dark grill marks.

2. Spread hummus on top of the grilled pita.

3. Top with feta, olives, cucumber, and tomato. Drizzle with olive oil.

4. Cut the pita into slices.

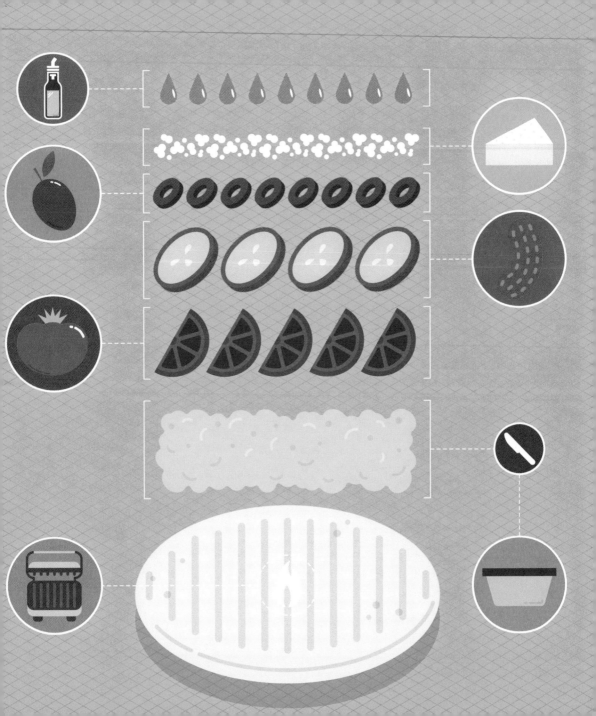

Scalloped Tomatoes

The name of the recipe sounds intimidating, but this dish is super simple — the perfect thing to make when you want Italian, and pasta is getting redundant. The bread, tomatoes, cheese and herbs combine to make a comforting stuffing-esque dish that makes me wonder why people don't eat stuffing year-round.

INGREDIENTS
- » Slice of crusty bread
- » Olive oil
- » Tomatoes *(sliced or cherry)*
- » Tomato sauce
- » Parmesan cheese
- » Oregano
- » Crushed red pepper flakes, *optional*

1. **Rip the bread into bite-size pieces** and put half the pieces in a bowl. Drizzle olive oil over the bread.

2. **Add half the tomatoes to the bowl.** Top the bread mixture with tomato sauce.

3. **Make another layer** with the remaining bread and tomatoes.

4. **Top the dish** with cheese, oregano, and crushed red pepper, if you'd like.

5. **Microwave** for about 2½ minutes.

Chicken and Waffles

If you have not tried the dreamy sweet and salty marriage of fried chicken, waffles, maple syrup, and barbecue sauce, you have not lived. Also, waffle makers are one of the best things to hit dining halls since soft-serve.

INGREDIENTS
>> Waffle batter
>> Fried chicken
>> Maple syrup
>> Barbecue sauce

EQUIPMENT
>> Waffle maker

1. **Make a waffle** in your dining hall's waffle maker.

2. **Put a piece of chicken or two on top** of the waffle.

3. **Drizzle equal parts** maple syrup and barbecue sauce over the entire dish.

CHOOSE YOUR CHICKEN
There are a lot of variations of chicken you can use in this dish. If your dining hall isn't offering fried chicken, try pulled chicken, grilled chicken breast, chicken drumsticks, or even chicken nuggets; they all work fine.

Cheese and Mushroom "Polenta"

I love cheesy mushroom polenta (polenta = the Italian version of grits). Unfortunately, polenta is not an ingredient you would commonly find in a dining hall, but you can substitute oatmeal for polenta and get the same hearty taste and texture. Now I am convinced that savory oatmeal is the next big thing — beyond mushrooms and cheese, there are almost endless possibilities for add-ins.

INGREDIENTS
>> Sliced mushrooms
>> Salt and pepper
>> Grated cheese
   (cheddar or Parmesan work well)
>> Bowl of oatmeal
>> Olive oil

EQUIPMENT
>> Microwave or sauté bar

1. **Cook the mushrooms** by either microwaving them on a plate with salt, pepper, and a little water, or sautéing them if you have access to a sauté bar.

2. **Mix a few heaping spoonfuls of grated cheese** into the oatmeal; stir until the cheese is melted and fully incorporated.

3. **Top the oatmeal** with the cooked mushrooms and drizzle olive oil and a little extra cheese on top.

Spanish Rice

My love affair with Spanish rice began at my elementary school cafeteria, and to this day I order my fajitas with double rice instead of rice and beans. I sometimes melt cheese on top of the rice, because since when did covering anything with cheese not make it taste better?

INGREDIENTS
>> Bowl of rice
>> Tomato sauce
>> Chili powder *(or any kind of hot sauce or chili sauce)*
>> Corn
>> Lemon wedges, *optional*
>> Salt and Pepper

EQUIPMENT
>> Microwave

1. **Mix a little bit of tomato sauce** plus a sprinkle of chili powder into the rice and stir in the corn.

2. **Microwave for 30 seconds,** or until everything is nice and hot.

3. **Spritz a little bit of lemon juice on top,** if you'd like, and season with salt and pepper.

Satay

The most critical element of satay, which is essentially grilled meat on a skewer, is the peanut sauce. I like my sauce really spicy and just a little sweet, but you can adjust the flavors to suit your personal tastes.

INGREDIENTS

>> Peanut butter
>> Chili sauce
>> Soy sauce
>> Yogurt

>> Sugar
>> PYOP *(pick your own protein)*
>> Olive oil
>> Chili powder

1. **Combine a few big spoonfuls** of peanut butter, a few squirts of chili sauce, and some soy sauce in a bowl. Whisk with a fork until the mixture is smooth.

2. **Add a little bit of yogurt and sugar.** You can add more or less of any of these ingredients depending on your tastes.

3. **Put your protein pick on a plate** and drizzle a little olive oil and chili powder over the top; dip your protein into the peanut sauce.

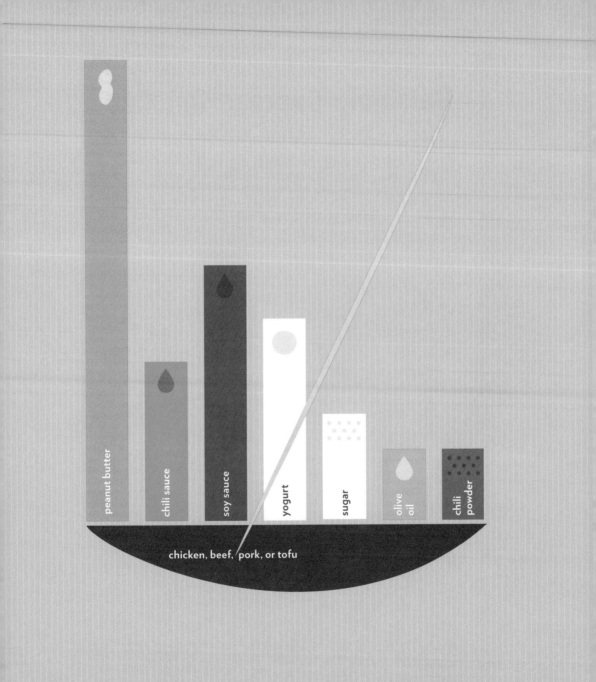

peanut butter

chili sauce

soy sauce

yogurt

sugar

olive oil

chili powder

chicken, beef, pork, or tofu

Balsamic Caprese Chicken

There's an almost infinite number of dishes that you can make "caprese" style by adding tomatoes and mozzarella, but this caprese chicken is definitely one of my favorites. Try this same combination on a burger, with eggs, or stuffed in an avocado. My basic rule of thumb: throw virtually anything over tomatoes, mozzarella, and maybe some pesto, and you will pretty much always be satisfied.

INGREDIENTS

» Balsamic vinegar
» Olive oil
» Sugar
» Grilled chicken

» Mozzarella
» Tomato slice
» Pesto

1. Mix together balsamic vinegar, olive oil, and a pinch of sugar in a bowl.

2. Drizzle half the dressing over a piece of grilled chicken.

3. Top the chicken with a piece of mozzarella, the tomato slice, and some pesto.

4. Drizzle the rest of the dressing on top of the mozzarella.

Ratatouille Baked Potato

Thanks to the Disney-Pixar movie, everyone is probably familiar with ratatouille, the French vegetable stew. But though it may be a stew, it has some great saucelike qualities. Don't believe me? Pour it over a baked sweet potato.

INGREDIENTS

>> Bowl of vegetables
   (typically zucchini, onion, eggplant, bell pepper — as few or as many of these as you want)

>> Tomato sauce

>> Baked sweet potato
   (Baked potatoes also work fine.)

EQUIPMENT

>> Microwave

1. **Top the vegetables** with a generous amount of tomato sauce.

2. **Microwave for about 2 minutes,** or until the vegetables are soft.

3. **Cut an incision into the potato,** and spoon the ratatouille inside.

Salad Pizza

I first discovered the joys of salad pizza with my friend Thea at Abbot's Pizza in Venice Beach, California — it is a great way to add a little extra oomph to a plain piece of pizza. You can eat the salad first, and then eat the dressing-soaked pizza. Alternatively, you can make each bite a combination of salad and pizza. Both are great, and they're even better if you spread sour cream on the base.

INGREDIENTS

» Salad *(You can make whatever salad you would like here, but I prefer using a Greek salad. Make sure the salad is thoroughly dressed.)*

» Pizza slice *(I prefer to use cheese.)*

» Grilled salmon or chicken, *optional*

1. Spread salad on pizza.

2. Top with grilled salmon or chicken, if you'd like.

3. Either eat the salad first, and then eat the pizza, or take a bite with everything on it.

Shakshouka

Shakshouka is an Israeli egg dish that is fantastic beyond the fact that it is such a fun word to say. It's spicy, it's hearty, and you can eat it at any time of the day.

INGREDIENTS
>> Tomato sauce
>> Jalapenos
>> Crushed red pepper flakes
>> Over-easy eggs
>> Feta cheese

1. **Put a few ladles of tomato sauce in a bowl** and mix in as many jalapenos and shakes of red pepper flakes as you are comfortable with.

2. **Place the eggs** on the tomato sauce.

3. **Sprinkle** with feta.

Tofu Scramble

When the dining hall is no longer serving breakfast, crumbled tofu can be a totally acceptable and actually quite tasty substitute for scrambled eggs, especially alongside lots of vegetables and a punchy soy-garlic sauce.

INGREDIENTS
>> Tofu
>> Vegetables of your choice (*I like mushrooms, bell peppers, and broccoli.*)
>> Soy sauce
>> Garlic powder
>> Chili sauce, *optional*

EQUIPMENT
>> Microwave

1. **Crumble the tofu in a bowl** with a fork or your hands. Add the vegetables to the bowl of tofu.

2. **Toss the vegetables and tofu** with soy sauce and a few shakes of garlic powder.

3. **Microwave for about 2 minutes,** or until the vegetables are tender. You may want to add a little extra soy sauce and some chili sauce before you eat.

Chicken Pot Pie

Chicken pot pie is an all-American dish that, ironically, I tried for the first time during my study-abroad term in France when one of my college friends made it for me. Of all the great meals I had in France, it may have been one of the best things I ate. Garlic bread works really well as the "crust" of the pie in this dining hall version.

INGREDIENTS

» Sliced chicken
» Mushrooms
» Corn
» Peas
» Alfredo sauce
» Garlic powder or oil
» Salt and pepper
» Garlic bread (or regular bread + garlic powder)

EQUIPMENT

» Toaster
» Microwave

1. Put the chicken, mushrooms, corn, peas, and Alfredo sauce in a bowl, and then sprinkle a little garlic powder or oil over the whole thing.

2. Add a few shakes of salt and pepper.

3. Toast the bread.

4. Break the bread into smaller pieces and arrange them like a crust over the chicken and vegetables.

5. Microwave the chicken pot pie for 30 seconds.

SNACKS

select

PYOP

MEAT or **VEGGIE**

asian lettuce
wraps \ page 86

select

PORK or **FISH**

select

southern poutine \ page 91

salmon spread \ page 95

asian nachos \ page 84

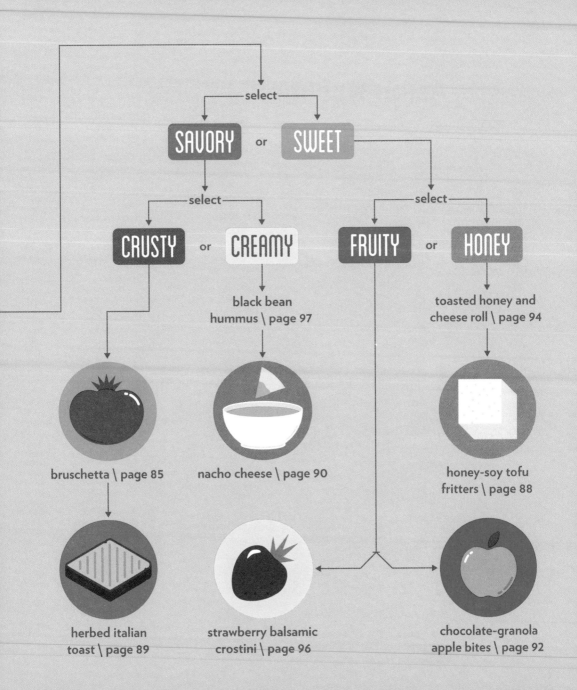

select

SAVORY or **SWEET**

select

CRUSTY or **CREAMY**

select

FRUITY or **HONEY**

black bean
hummus \ page 97

toasted honey and
cheese roll \ page 94

bruschetta \ page 85

nacho cheese \ page 90

honey-soy tofu
fritters \ page 88

herbed italian
toast \ page 89

strawberry balsamic
crostini \ page 96

chocolate-granola
apple bites \ page 92

Asian Nachos

Who said cheese is the only thing you can put on top of tortilla chips? Not only does the combination of sashimi, avocado, ginger, and chili sauce taste amazing on chips, but also this dish is just really nice to look at. And as an annoying restaurant coworker once told me, you eat with your eyes first!

INGREDIENTS

» Plate of tortilla chips
» Any kind of sashimi *(I prefer salmon.)*
» Avocado *(Chunks or slices work fine.)*
» Sushi toppings of your choice *(recommended: ginger, wasabi, chili sauce, sweet soy sauce, lemon)*

1. **Layer the sashimi and avocado on top** of the chips such that they are evenly distributed.

2. **Add toppings of your choice.** I suggest drizzling sweet soy sauce and chili sauce (or chili mayo, if your dining hall has it), then dotting the nachos with a little wasabi (don't go too crazy!) and a few pieces of ginger. Finish with a spritz of lemon.

Bruschetta

Even though many people — including myself until recently — pronounce the name of this dish incorrectly (it is, in fact, pronounced Bru-ske-ta), bruschetta is a universally loved Italian antipasto. This recipe is very simple, as it can be made pretty much entirely out of salad bar ingredients, but it packs a flavorful punch.

INGREDIENTS
» Bread *(the crustier, the better)*
» Olive oil
» Tomatoes
» Balsamic vinegar
» Lemon wedge
» Salt and pepper
» Mozzarella, *optional*

EQUIPMENT
» Panini press or toaster

1. **Grill a piece of bread** in a panini press (or you can toast it) and drizzle it with olive oil.

2. **Put some chopped tomatoes in a bowl** with a little bit of balsamic vinegar, the juice of one lemon wedge, and salt and pepper.

3. **Put mozzarella on the bread,** if you'd like, and spoon the tomato mixture over the top.

BRUSCHETTA
Bruschetta is very easy to modify according to your preferences or the ingredients at your disposal. I like using basil or sun-dried tomato pesto as a base or adding chopped red bell peppers or onions.

Asian Lettuce Wraps

This is a tale of two lettuces. The first is the tasteless, shredded lettuce you get in the salad bar that doesn't really do much by way of actually enhancing a dish. And then there are the big, crisp lettuce cups you can usually find in the sandwich line that, when used as a wrap alongside a spicy Asian dipping sauce, can be so satisfying at any part of the day.

INGREDIENTS

- Lettuce leaves
- Bean sprouts
- Sliced carrots
- PYOP *(pick your own protein)*
- Soy sauce
- Chili sauce

1. **Lay the lettuce leaves flat** on a plate and top each one with bean sprouts, carrots, and your protein pick.

2. **Roll the lettuce leaves up** into wraps.

3. **In a small bowl, combine equal parts** soy sauce and chili sauce. Use this as a dipping sauce for the wraps.

SAUCE OPTIONS

Many dining halls offer different kinds of Asian sauces. I also like dipping these wraps in Thai peanut sauce or sweet and sour sauce.

Honey-Soy Tofu Fritters

Tofu often gets a bad reputation in the food world as bland and soggy, but giving it a crunchy exterior and a sweet and salty coating could be just the thing to change the minds of tofu skeptics everywhere.

INGREDIENTS
» Honey
» Soy sauce
» Cooked tofu (*in chunks*)
» Croutons

1. Put honey and soy sauce (a little more honey, a little less soy sauce) into a bowl and stir the two together.

2. Add the tofu chunks to the sauce and roll them around so that they are evenly coated.

3. Crush croutons in a separate bowl and transfer the tofu into the bowl of crushed croutons. Roll the tofu around such that each piece gets a crouton crust.

4. Transfer the tofu to a plate, and drizzle the rest of the sauce on top.

Herbed Italian Toast

My mother invented this recipe at home as a way to dress up even the plainest and most tasteless piece of bread, and I probably made it at least once a day in college. It makes for a very flavorful complement to a cup of soup or a salad.

INGREDIENTS

» Bread
» Olive oil
» Dried herbs and spices
  (recommended: oregano, basil, crushed red pepper flakes)
» Salt and pepper
» Parmesan cheese, *optional*

EQUIPMENT

» Toaster

1. Toast the bread.

2. Drizzle olive oil on the toasted bread.

3. Sprinkle on herbs, salt and pepper, and Parmesan, if you'd like.

**CHEESY
GOODNESS**

Nacho cheese
is a versa-
tile sauce
that works
with plenty
more than
just chips.
Try dipping
pretzels into
it, or put it
on a hot dog,
hamburger, or
chili. Veggie
haters: nacho
cheese over
broccoli may
just be your
next big
breakthrough.

Nacho Cheese (Queso)

I don't know why nacho cheese seems to only be found at mediocre Mexican restaurants and sporting events. It is heartier than salsa and more flavorful than just melted cheese on chips. Plus, in this version, you get to see the cheese come out of the microwave all hot and bubbly.

INGREDIENTS
» Grated cheddar cheese
» Salsa
» Butter

1. **Put a few heaping spoonfuls of cheese** in a bowl and add enough salsa to thoroughly coat the cheese.

2. **Stir in two spoonfuls** of butter.

3. **Microwave for two minutes,** stirring halfway through.

Southern Poutine

Poutine is a Canadian dish made with French fries covered in gravy and cheese curds. I didn't like it until I tried it with the gravy swapped out for barbecue sauce, which provides a sweet and tangy complement to the melted cheese and fries.

INGREDIENTS
>> Grated cheese *(I prefer cheddar.)*
>> Plate of French fries
>> Pulled chicken or pulled pork, *optional*
>> Barbecue sauce

EQUIPMENT
>> Microwave

1. **Sprinkle a generous amount of grated cheese** over the fries, and microwave until the cheese melts.

2. **Add meat,** if you'd like, and drizzle barbecue sauce over the top.

Chocolate-Granola Apple Bites

Apple slices are a great snack, but they get boring fast. Take them to the next level by coating them with peanut butter, granola, and chocolate chips for a sweet energizing bite.

INGREDIENTS
>> Peanut butter
>> Plate of apple slices
>> Granola
>> Chocolate chips

1. Spread peanut butter on one side of each apple slice.

2. Crust each slice with granola and chocolate chips.

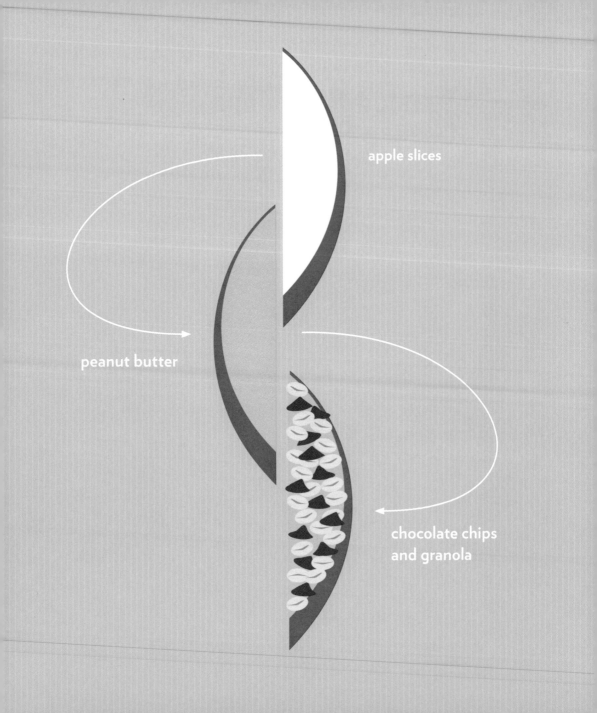

apple slices

peanut butter

chocolate chips
and granola

Toasted Honey and Cheese Roll

One of the most basic snacks in existence is a bread roll with butter — but you can make things a lot more interesting by substituting cheese and honey for the butter.

INGREDIENTS

>> Bread roll

>> Spreadable cheese
(Goat cheese and cream cheese both work well.)

>> Honey

EQUIPMENT

>> Toaster

1. Toast the bread roll.

2. Cut the roll in half and spread the cheese on both halves.

3. Drizzle honey on each side.

Salmon Spread

I was always super skeptical about the idea of a spread with salmon in it, but this version — which is bright, a little chunky, and a little spicy — definitely changed my mind. You can't go wrong spreading this over a toasted bagel as a nice variation on lox.

INGREDIENTS
>> Grilled salmon
>> Cream cheese
>> Dijon mustard
>> Lemon wedges
>> Salt and pepper

1. **Flake the salmon** into a bowl.

2. **Add a few spoonfuls** of cream cheese, a squirt of mustard, and a little bit of lemon juice.

3. **Season with a few shakes** of salt and pepper and stir to combine.

Strawberry Balsamic Crostini

It's hard to decide if this is a snack or a dessert, but trust me when I say that the syrupy and slightly sweet flavor of balsamic-coated strawberries tastes incredible over creamy cheese and crusty bread.

INGREDIENTS
» Crusty bread
» Strawberries
» Honey
» Balsamic vinegar
» Spreadable cheese
(Goat cheese and cream cheese both work well.)

EQUIPMENT
» Toaster
» Microwave

1. **Toast the bread** and cut it into a few mini-toasts.

2. **Mix strawberries,** a few squeezes of honey, and a little bit of balsamic vinegar together and microwave for 90 seconds.

3. **Spread cheese on the toasts** and top them with the strawberries.

Black Bean Hummus

Black bean hummus is a more flavorful, easier-to-use version of black beans, and the options for this spread are infinite. Layer it into a burrito, add it to a sandwich, or just enjoy it as a dip for raw veggies.

INGREDIENTS
- » Bowl of black beans
- » Olive oil
- » Lime *(Lemon would also work.)*
- » Garlic powder
- » Chili powder
- » Salt and pepper

1. Mash the black beans with a fork.

2. Stir in enough olive oil to give the dip a creamy consistency.

3. Add a little lime juice and a few shakes of garlic powder, chili powder, salt, and pepper. Stir to combine.

DESSERTS

select

NO DAIRY or **DAIRY**

select

FRUITY or **CHOCOLATE**

PUDDING or **ICE CREAM** or

banana boats \ page 112

banana crumble
page 102

s'mores cereal
treats \ page 116

banana pudding \ page 100

chocolate bread
pudding \ page 104

pb&j sundae \ page 121

olive oil chocolate
ice cream sundae \ page 111

chocolate chip cookie
dough \ page 110

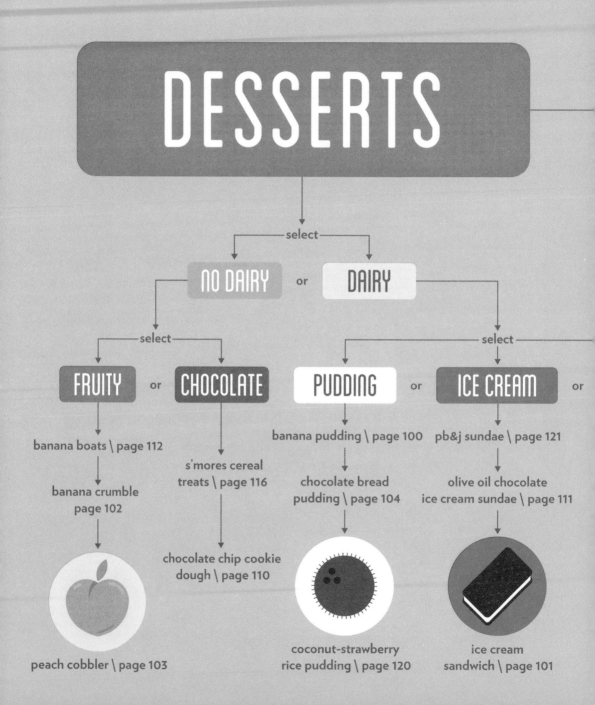

peach cobbler \ page 103

coconut-strawberry
rice pudding \ page 120

ice cream
sandwich \ page 101

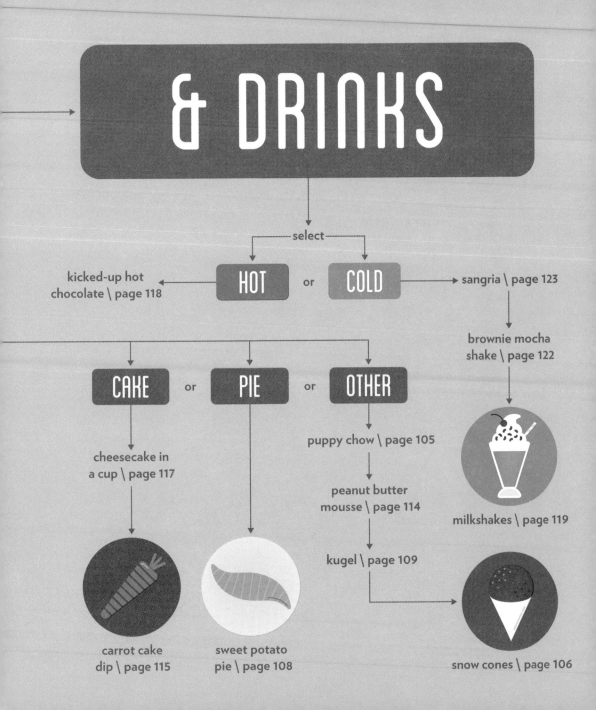

& DRINKS

select

HOT or **COLD**

kicked-up hot chocolate \ page 118

sangria \ page 123

brownie mocha shake \ page 122

CAKE or **PIE** or **OTHER**

cheesecake in a cup \ page 117

puppy chow \ page 105

peanut butter mousse \ page 114

kugel \ page 109

milkshakes \ page 119

carrot cake dip \ page 115

sweet potato pie \ page 108

snow cones \ page 106

Banana Pudding

I never quite understood the traditional banana pudding — the kind with vanilla wafers, whipped cream, and custard — so I came up with this version with banana chunks, yogurt, cinnamon, and honey. For a healthy dessert, it's pretty gratifying.

INGREDIENTS
» Banana
» Yogurt *(I recommend plain or vanilla.)*
» Honey
» Cinnamon

1. **Mash up a banana** in a bowl with a fork.

2. **Mix in yogurt,** a few squirts of honey, and a shake or two of cinnamon until the whole mixture resembles a smooth pudding.

Ice Cream Sandwich

A basic ice cream sandwich features ice cream between two cookies or wafers, but having ice cream between cake puts the dessert sandwich on a whole new plane. Make your sandwich extra decadent and roll it in crushed Oreos or mini M&Ms. I dare you.

INGREDIENTS

>> Pound cake or brownie

>> Soft-serve ice cream

>> Extra fillings of your choice: peanut butter, jam, chocolate sauce, crushed Oreos, cinnamon

1. **Cut the pound cake or brownie in half horizontally,** so that you have two thinner pieces.

2. **Top one of the halves** with ice cream.

3. **Add your favorite fillings,** and then press the two halves together.

CRUSHED TOPPINGS

If your ice cream bar does not offer pre-crushed toppings, like Oreos, here is an easy way to crush them: grab a takeout bag or unfold a napkin, put your topping of choice inside and crush it with your hands from the outside of the bag. You'll get perfectly crushed toppings without any mess.

Banana Crumble

This was yet another amazing dessert I discovered while studying abroad in France, and it completely reversed my perception that crumbles are only for apples. I can honestly say that I have late-night cravings for this dish — the banana-cinnamon-granola-salt combo is completely unexpected but works so well.

INGREDIENTS
» Banana
» Cinnamon
» Honey
» Granola
» Salt
» Vanilla ice cream or yogurt

EQUIPMENT
» Microwave

1. **Use a knife or your hands** to divide a banana into small pieces in a cup.

2. **Top the banana with generous doses** of cinnamon, honey, and granola. The bananas should be entirely coated.

3. **Add a few small shakes of salt,** and then microwave for 2 minutes.

4. **Spoon the banana mixture** over vanilla ice cream or yogurt.

Peach Cobbler

This recipe is particularly awesome because (1) peach cobbler is fantastic, and (2) this version uses oatmeal as a base, so you can very acceptably eat peach cobbler for both breakfast and dessert. High fives all around!

INGREDIENTS

>> Bowl of sliced peaches
(Frozen or canned work fine; fresh are best.)

>> Oatmeal

>> Brown sugar

>> Granola

>> Butter

EQUIPMENT

>> Microwave

1. **Top the peaches** with a generous amount of oatmeal.

2. **Mix brown sugar into the oatmeal mixture,** and then add a little more brown sugar on top.

3. **Top the oatmeal** with a layer of granola and a little butter.

4. **Microwave** for about 45 seconds.

Chocolate Bread Pudding

This bread pudding recipe has the ultimate soak factor, meaning that the bread absorbs all of the milk to create a truly melt-in-your-mouth dessert. If chocolate isn't your thing, check the sidebar for a great alternative, Apple Cinnamon Bread Pudding.

INGREDIENTS

» Thick slice of bread

» Chocolate soy milk
(Regular chocolate milk also works fine.)

» Ice cream, *optional*

EQUIPMENT

» Microwave

1. **Break the bread into pieces** in a bowl.

2. **Douse the bread with chocolate soy milk,** until the bread is swimming in the milk but not drowning in it (the milk should cover the bread by about a centimeter).

3. **Microwave for a little more than a minute,** or until all the soy milk soaks into the bread.

4. **Top with ice cream,** if you'd like.

APPLE CINNAMON BREAD PUDDING

This is one of my all-time favorite variations. Just swap out the chocolate milk for regular milk or vanilla soy milk, and then add applesauce and a little honey and cinnamon.

Puppy Chow

Puppy chow is an addictive mixture of chocolate- and peanut butter-coated cereal that you can easily make in big batches at your dining hall and keep in your dorm room as a snack — but there's also a good chance you'll eat most of it on your walk home.

INGREDIENTS

>> Peanut butter
>> Chocolate sauce or chocolate syrup
>> Any kind of Chex-like cereal *(I recommend Rice Chex or Crispix.)*
>> Instant hot chocolate powder

EQUIPMENT

>> Microwave

1. **Combine equal parts** peanut butter and chocolate sauce in a bowl and microwave for about 20 seconds, or until the mixture starts to reach a more liquid consistency.

2. **Put cereal in any kind of takeout bag or box** and pour the chocolate and peanut butter sauce on top.

3. **Toss the sauce and the cereal together** in the bag or box so that the cereal is evenly and fully coated.

4. **Add hot chocolate powder** and keep tossing and shaking the cereal until you have added enough powder to coat the cereal. You should be left with bite-size clusters.

Snow Cones

I love snow cones because they are like summer in a cup. If you don't have crushed ice at your dining hall, you can crush the ice in a blender if you have a smoothie station. I like adding gummy bears into my snow cone (a little inspiration from my fifth-grade-literature-teacher-turned-snow-cone vendor) to get a chewy surprise with each bite.

INGREDIENTS
» Ice (crushed, if you have it)
» Fruit punch
» Sugar
» Gummy bears, optional

EQUIPMENT
» Ice machine or blender

1. **If the ice is not already crushed,** process it in a blender and put it in a soup cup, mounding it up higher than the rim.

2. **Get a small cup** of your favorite fruit punch and add a few packets of sugar to it.

3. **Pour the fruit punch over the crushed ice.** Only pour a little bit, otherwise you will just have fruit punch in a bowl.

4. **Push a gummy bear** (or more) into the center of the snow cone, if you'd like.

Sweet Potato Pie

Thanksgiving is my favorite day of the year, because there is really nothing not to love about an entire holiday centered on a food-coma-inducing dinner — especially one produced by my mother. This deconstructed version of the classic Thanksgiving dessert works more like a parfait than a pie, but it still has all of the best flavors of the fall.

INGREDIENTS

» Sweet potato
» Butter
» Brown sugar
» Cinnamon cereal
(I recommend Cracklin' Oat Bran or Cinnamon Toast Crunch.)

» Vanilla yogurt or ice cream

EQUIPMENT

» Microwave

1. **Scoop the flesh out of the sweet potato** and mash in a bowl.

2. **Stir a few spoonfuls** of butter and brown sugar into the sweet potato, and then microwave for about 45 seconds, until the butter has melted.

3. **Crumble the cinnamon cereal** on top of the sweet potato.

4. **Top with a thin layer** of brown sugar and a dollop of vanilla yogurt or ice cream.

Kugel

I was introduced to kugel, a sweet noodle dish, by my freshman year college roommate, who would bring it from home. I snuck a few bites, decided I was a big fan of the cinnamon-sugar-noodles combo, and came up with this version so I could enjoy it whenever I wanted.

INGREDIENTS

» Bowl of pasta *(Egg noodles work best if they are available.)*
» Cottage cheese
» Brown sugar
» Raisins
» Cinnamon

EQUIPMENT

» Microwave

1. Mix pasta with an equal amount of cottage cheese.

2. Stir in a generous amount of brown sugar and raisins, plus a few healthy shakes of cinnamon.

3. Microwave the dish for about 2 minutes.

Chocolate Chip Cookie Dough

Cookie dough is one of those foods that you are fully aware is not just unhealthy, but hazardous, yet you eat it anyway for the short-term satisfaction. This cookie dough recipe is different, though, because it is just as decadent as regular cookie dough but will not give you Salmonella. It is even pretty healthy! It truly is a dessert miracle.

INGREDIENTS

- » Banana
- » Muesli or oats
- » Peanut butter
- » Chocolate chips
- » Cinnamon
- » Salt

1. Mash half of a banana in a bowl with a fork.

2. Add a big handful of muesli or oats and a spoonful of peanut butter to the banana. Add chocolate chips and cinnamon to your taste.

3. Finish with a pinch of salt.

4. Mix the whole dish together and eat with a spoon or in bite-size chunks.

Olive Oil Chocolate Ice Cream Sundae

I saw this pairing on the Food Network and thought it sounded absolutely bizarre. I tried it anyway and discovered that the ice cream totally transforms the olive oil, giving it this amazing sweetness. For the best results, use a super-dark chocolate ice cream.

INGREDIENTS
» Dark chocolate ice cream
» Whipped cream
» Olive oil
» Salt

1. **Put a scoop of ice cream** in one side of a bowl, and then put whipped cream on the other side.

2. **Drizzle a little bit of olive oil** over both the ice cream and the whipped cream.

3. **Add a very small shake of salt** to the sundae — this will really tie all the flavors together. Dip your spoon into the ice cream and then the whipped cream for each bite.

Banana Boats

I like this dessert a lot because of the novelty of eating it right out of the banana peel. Plus, the banana and toppings get all gooey when they mix and mingle in the microwave. You'll never eat a plain banana again.

INGREDIENTS

» Banana
» Toppings of your choice *(Great options include coconut shavings, chocolate chips, granola, nuts, or M&Ms.)*

EQUIPMENT

» Microwave

1. **Use a knife to make a slit** in the banana peel by cutting it down the length of one side. Use your fingers to slightly pull open the top of the banana. Do not remove the peel.

2. **Fill the banana** with your toppings.

3. **Microwave the banana** for 30 seconds at a time about three times, or until the peel is dark and the toppings are slightly melted.

4. **To eat, use a spoon** to scoop the filling out of the peel.

Peanut Butter Mousse

This is one of the most amazing uses of cottage cheese that I have ever encountered. It combines with peanut butter to make a smooth, tangy, and sweet mousse. For peanut butter lovers, there is no better dessert.

INGREDIENTS

>> Bowl of cottage cheese
>> Smooth peanut butter
>> Sugar packet

1. Add peanut butter to the cottage cheese; you want a little less peanut butter than cottage cheese.

2. Add a packet of sugar.

3. Mix vigorously with a spoon until everything is thoroughly combined.

Carrot Cake Dip

Carrot cake is one of my favorite sweets, but it's not something you can just whip up in a dining hall. Thankfully, it translates quite well into a dip. Spread it on a cookie or a graham cracker for the total cake experience.

INGREDIENTS
» Bowl of shredded carrots
» Brown sugar
» Raisins
» Orange juice
» Cinnamon
» Vanilla yogurt
» Graham crackers or sugar cookies

EQUIPMENT
» Microwave

1. **Mix a few spoonfuls of brown sugar,** a spoonful of raisins, and a little bit of orange juice and cinnamon into the bowl of carrots.

2. **Microwave for no more than 1 minute** — just enough to soften the carrots.

3. **Stir in a few spoonfuls** of yogurt.

4. **Spread on graham crackers** or sugar cookies.

S'mores Cereal Treats

It's s'mores without the campfire. And you get the added bonus of getting to watch the marshmallows inflate in the microwave as they mold almost perfectly into each crevice of the chocolate cereal. That's what I call dinner and a show.

INGREDIENTS
» Bowl of chocolate puff cereal (*I recommend Cocoa Puffs.*)
» Marshmallows

EQUIPMENT
» Microwave

1. Top the cereal with an equal quantity of marshmallows.

2. Microwave for 1 minute.

3. Let the treats sit for 30 seconds before digging in with either a spoon or your hands.

Cheesecake in a Cup

If you like cheesecake at all, this is a game-changing dessert. Digging your spoon down into each layer and getting the perfect bite of cream cheese, cookie, and jam is nothing short of orgasmic.

INGREDIENTS
- » Cream cheese
- » Brown Sugar
- » Cookie *(I prefer sugar cookies, but any simple, vanilla-flavored cookie will work.)*
- » Jam *(I prefer strawberry.)*

1. **Mix a few spoonfuls of cream cheese** and a small spoonful of brown sugar in a mug.

2. **Spread the cream cheese mixture** on the cookie and place it back in the mug.

3. **Top with jam.**

KICKED-UP HOT CHOCOLATE

A cup of hot chocolate is so satisfying on a cold, winter's day, but there are plenty of easy ways to make it much more exciting.

START WITH
A CUP OF
STEAMING HOT
CHOCOLATE
AND ADD . . .

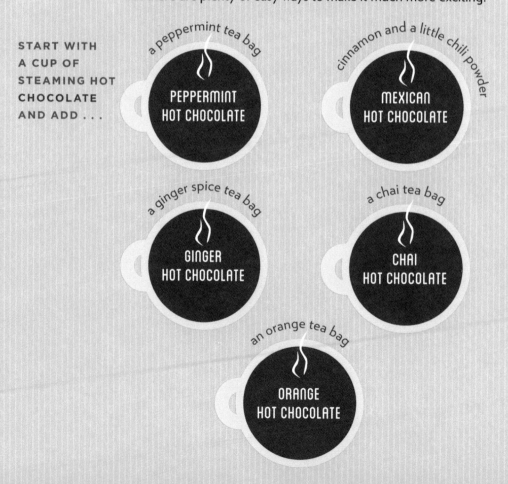

a peppermint tea bag

PEPPERMINT
HOT CHOCOLATE

cinnamon and a little chili powder

MEXICAN
HOT CHOCOLATE

a ginger spice tea bag

GINGER
HOT CHOCOLATE

a chai tea bag

CHAI
HOT CHOCOLATE

an orange tea bag

ORANGE
HOT CHOCOLATE

MILKSHAKES

I am embarrassed to say that I have never been able to finish an entire milkshake by myself, but I'd like to think that's why you always see people splitting one milkshake with two straws in comics from the 1960s. Finish this milkshake by yourself if you can handle the brain freeze, but if not, you can make it a two-straw job for sure.

INGREDIENTS
» Soft serve ice cream or frozen yogurt *(any flavor)*
» Milk
» Mix-ins, *optional (some suggestions: M&Ms, Oreos, Reese's Pieces — basically anything you could find in a McFlurry)*

1. **Put two scoops of ice cream** in a cup and add enough milk to almost cover the ice cream.

2. **Use a spoon to blend the ingredients** together by mashing the ice cream against the side of the cup until the mixture is smooth.

3. **Top with** your favorite mix-ins.

Coconut-Strawberry Rice Pudding

This cooling rice pudding is somewhat inspired by the classic Thai dessert, mango sticky rice, but it uses strawberries, vanilla yogurt, and shredded coconut, which you can usually find in an ice cream toppings bar. It is a fantastic hot-weather dessert.

INGREDIENTS

» Bowl of rice
» Vanilla yogurt
» Shredded sweetened coconut
» Strawberries

1. Mix a few spoonfuls of yogurt and a big handful of shredded coconut into the rice.

2. Garnish with sliced strawberries on top.

PB&J Sundae

I am a peanut butter and jelly addict. I have had this killer combination in cupcakes, in cakes, in doughnuts, and in muffins. There is not a single dessert in which it has not tasted phenomenal. You don't even really need the frozen yogurt in this recipe, but using it will get you fewer "judgy" looks.

INGREDIENTS
» Vanilla frozen yogurt (or ice cream)
» Peanut butter
» Strawberry jelly (Raspberry is fine too; grape is for fools.)

1. **Top a bowl of vanilla frozen yogurt** with a few spoonfuls each of peanut butter and strawberry jelly.

2. **Swirl the peanut butter and jelly** lightly into the frozen yogurt with a spoon.

Brownie Mocha Shake

If you are trying to shake your coffee addiction, you should probably skip to the next recipe, because the only thing more addictive than iced coffee is iced coffee blended up with brownie bits.

INGREDIENTS
» Large cup of cold coffee
» Milk
» Brownie

EQUIPMENT
» Blender, *optional*

1. **Add a little** ice and milk to the coffee.

2. **Break up a brownie** into small pieces and add the pieces to the coffee.

3. **If you have a blender,** blend everything just until the shake is mostly smooth but a few brownie chunks are still visible. If you don't have a blender, mix everything with a spoon until the brownie has soaked fully into the coffee and milk.

Sangria

Sangria is usually one of those drinks that you have to let sit for a couple of hours, but when you take wine out of the picture, you can quickly transport yourself back to your study-abroad term in Spain with a little seltzer, juice, and whatever fruits you have on hand.

INGREDIENTS

>> Tall glass of punch or juice *(I prefer mango or orange.)*
>> Seltzer or Sprite
>> Sliced fruit *(You can use whatever is available, but berries usually work best.)*
>> Lemon wedges

1. **Add a few splashes** of seltzer or Sprite to the juice.

2. **Float the** sliced fruit and lemon wedges in the glass.

INDEX

OTHER STOREY TITLES